INTRODUCTION TO
PRESOCRATICS

INTRODUCTION TO
PRESOCRATICS

A THEMATIC APPROACH TO EARLY GREEK PHILOSOPHY WITH KEY READINGS

GIANNIS STAMATELLOS

WILEY-BLACKWELL

A John Wiley & Sons, Ltd., Publication

This edition first published 2012
© 2012 John Wiley & Sons, Inc.

Wiley-Blackwell is an imprint of John Wiley & Sons, formed by the merger
of Wiley's global Scientific, Technical and Medical business with
Blackwell Publishing.

Registered Office
John Wiley & Sons Ltd, The Atrium, Southern Gate, Chichester, West Sussex, PO19
8SQ, UK

Editorial Offices
350 Main Street, Malden, MA 02148-5020, USA
9600 Garsington Road, Oxford, OX4 2DQ, UK
The Atrium, Southern Gate, Chichester, West Sussex, PO19 8SQ, UK

For details of our global editorial offices, for customer services, and for information
about how to apply for permission to reuse the copyright material in this book please
see our website at www.wiley.com/wiley-blackwell.

The right of Giannis Stamatellos to be identified as the author of this work has been
asserted in accordance with the UK Copyright, Designs and Patents Act 1988.

Library of Congress Cataloging-in-Publication Data
Stamatellos, Giannis, 1970–
    Introduction to Presocratics : a thematic approach to early Greek philosophy with key
readings / Giannis Stamatellos.
        p. cm.
    Includes bibliographical references (p.   ) and indexes.
    ISBN 978-0-470-65502-3 (hardback : alk. paper) – ISBN 978-0-470-65503-0 (pbk.:
alk. paper)   1. Pre-Socratic philosophers.   I. Title.
    B187.5.S73 2012
    182–dc23

                                                            2011045995

A catalogue record for this book is available from the British Library.

Set in 10/12.5 pt Plantin by Toppan Best-set Premedia Limited
Printed in Malaysia by Ho Printing (M) Sdn Bhd

1   2012

To Rosemary

Contents

Preface

The origins of Western philosophy and science can be traced back to the early Greek philosophers of the sixth and fifth century BCE, known as 'Presocratics' – that is, those who preceded Socrates. The main figures are Thales, Anaximander and Anaximenes, all three from Miletus, on the Ionian coast of Asia Minor; the widely traveled Xenophanes of Colophon; Heraclitus of Ephesus; Pythagoras from the island of Samos; Parmenides and Zeno, known as 'Eleatics' on account of their origin from Elea in south Italy; Melissus from Samos, also placed among the Eleatics for his support and adaptation of Parmenides' arguments; and then, finally, the 'pluralists' (also called 'Neo-Ionians') – physicalists who posited more than one basic principle in their ontology: the Sicilian Empedocles; Anaxagoras of Clazomenae; and the 'atomists' – Leucippus and Democritus, both of them connected with Abdera in northern Greece.

This book aims to offer a concise philosophical introduction to the Presocratic thinkers and in doing so it follows a thematic exposition of the topics discussed by these Greek pioneers. It intends to show how Presocratic thinking formed, creating the early Greek philosophical tradition, and how one Presocratic responded to another. In this way it hopes to demonstrate their innovative philosophical explorations.

The book comprises of a series of short essays on six philosophical themes significant to Presocratic inquiry. The six themes are: *principles*, *the cosmos*, *being*, *soul*, *knowledge* and *ethics*. These themes emerge as important philosophical topics not only in the history of ancient Greek philosophy, but also in modern philosophical inquiries and they have been selected for this reason. They also indicate the wide range of philosophical interests found in the Presocratic tradition, which embraced the origins of cosmos and being, the nature of the soul, the foundation of human knowledge and the values of human life. However, as this is a short, introductory book, the analysis of each theme is not intended to be exhaustive. Nor are the selected themes the only ones discussed in the Presocratic tradition. Controversies that surround many of the issues related to Presocratic scholarship in each of these areas can only be hinted at, while signposts to further study can be found in the bibliography. Furthermore, this short study is of an introductory nature and the treatment of the six Presocratic themes is mainly doxographical. Hence this book does not address scholars and advanced students of ancient Greek philosophy; rather it targets non-experienced readers and people who are interested in Presocratic philosophy, hoping to motivate them into further reading and exploration of the early Greek philosophical tradition.

Within this framework, we begin with the role and importance of the Presocratic pioneers in ancient Greek philosophy and historiography (chapter 1); this is followed by a brief account of the life and work of individual thinkers (chapter 2). The first theme concerns the basic principles that the Presocratics postulated. Its presentation will take us into the material explanations of the Ionians, the Pythagorean apprehension of the formal principle, and the pluralistic approaches of Empedocles, Anaxagoras, Leucippus and Democritus (chapter 3). There follows a study of Presocratic cosmologies, contrasting the Ionian development of the Homeric image of the cosmos with the mathematical structure of the universe put forward by the Pythagoreans and with the pluralistic views of the universe that are found in later Presocratics (chapter 4). This leads into the subject of the nature of being itself, where particular emphasis will be placed on the main arguments of Parmenides' controversial denial of non-being in favor of a unified, timeless and indestructible being; on Zeno's famous paradoxes of motion and refutations of the plurality of being; and on Melissus' notion of the infinity of being (chapter 5). The concept of the soul as source of life and intelligence is our next theme, and it includes a brief discussion of transmigration, time and immortality (chapter 6). Then we shall explore pioneering work on epistemology, work based on the early discrimination between truth, knowledge and belief, which is fundamental in this field; and here we have included a brief account of the Presocratics' criticism of traditional polytheism, human knowledge and sense-perception (chapter 7). Chapter 8 is an introduction to Presocratic moral philosophy; it moves from the heroic ethics found in Homer to an early form of virtue ethics propounded by Heraclitus and Empedocles, and from there to Democritus' ethics. A general conclusion is offered as the ending chapter of the book (chapter 9).

A translation of the main fragments by Rosemary Wright is offered in Appendix A for general reference. Two other appendices have been added: one on the Presocratic sources (Appendix B) and another on the legacy and reception of Presocratic philosophy in later thought and traditions (Appendix C). Finally, the book is supplemented with a glossary of Greek terms, a glossary of philosophical terms, and, of course, a general bibliography and an index.

I owe special thanks to Professor Leo Catana and to the Center for Neoplatonic Virtue Ethics (University of Copenhagen) for offering me an academic environment for this project and the opportunity to discuss topics in detail. I am also grateful to Professor Andrew Smith, Dr. Dionysis Mentzeniotis, Professor Evangelos Roussos, Evita C. Alexopoulos and my friend, Kostas Andreou, for their advice, help and encouragement. I am thankful to my student, Costas Kalogeropoulos, for designing the map. I would also like to acknowledge the assistance I have received from Galen Smith and Haze Humbert of Wiley-Blackwell; I am grateful for their patience and attention throughout the production of this book. I also thank the anonymous reviewers, whose critical comments and insights have brought many improvements. My wife Alexandra, my daughter Antonia, my son Aristoteles and my mother Antonia provide, as always, unstinting love and care. The volume is dedicated to Rosemary Wright for her inspired teaching, philosophical motivation and unconditional support over the past twelve years.

Giannis Stamatellos

Chronology

Time (BCE)	Thinker	Birthplace
c. 800–750	Homer	Chios
c. 750–700	Hesiod	Ascra
born c. 600	Pherecydes	Syros
fl. c. 585	Thales	Miletus
fl. c. 550	Anaximander	Miletus
fl. c. 545	Anaximenes	Miletus
c. 570–483	Xenophanes	Colophon
fl. c. 540	Pythagoras	Samos
fl. c. 500	Heraclitus	Ephesus
c. 500–450	Alcmaeon	Croton
c. 470–385	Philolaus	Croton
fl. c. 480	Parmenides	Elea
fl. c. 450	Zeno	Elea
fl. c. 440	Melissus	Samos
c. 460	Empedocles	Acragas
c. 450	Anaxagoras	Clazomenae
fl. c. 450	Leucippus	Miletus (?)
born c. 460	Democritus	Abdera
born c. 440	Diogenes	Apollonia

Reference Guide to the Presocratics

The Diels–Kranz (DK) edition of 1951 is the standard reference work in the field of Presocratic scholarship. The DK numbering system has remained the standard way of referring to the Presocratics, and it has been followed in this book. Testimonies form the A section, and fragments form the B section. For each Presocratic, A section material includes ancient accounts of his life, writings and doctrines, and B section material consists of the extant texts (longer or shorter fragments from a work, or just a few words or phrases quoted by someone else). Individual fragments and testimonials are numbered sequentially – and so are individual philosophers, who are designated by their sequential number. For example, Thales is number 11 in Diels–Kranz, so a reference to the third testimonial concerning his life would take the form DK 11A3.

In this book, for the sake of brevity, when a Presocratic is under discussion (or has already been named), this type of reference will be abbreviated to its A or B part; so DK 11A3 will become Thales A3, or simply A3. However, to make it easier for readers to connect quickly to the DK edition and find the reference in question easily, we attach here an alphabetical list of concordances between each name and the corresponding number in DK:

Alcmaeon	24 (vol. 1)
Anaxagoras	59 (vol. 2)
Anaximander	12 (vol. 1)
Anaximenes	13 (vol. 1)
Archytas	47 (vol. 1)
Democritus	68 (vol. 2)
Diogenes	64 (vol. 2)
Empedocles	31 (vol. 1)

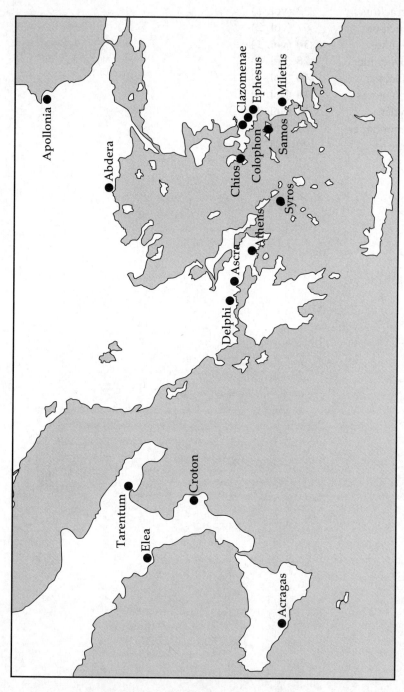

The Eastern Mediterranean in the Sixth and Fifth Century BCE

1

INTRODUCTION

Introduction

'Ancient Greek philosophy' is the general phrase used for the philosophical explorations of Greek thinkers who flourished approximately
between the sixth century BCE and the sixth century CE. It is usually
divided, conventionally, into four historical periods:

1   the *Presocratic* period (*c.* sixth to fifth century BCE)
2   the *classical* period (*c.* late fifth to fourth century BCE)
3   the *Hellenistic* period (*c.* late fourth to first century BCE)
4   the *late Hellenistic and Roman* period, which extends far into late
    antiquity (*c.* first century BCE to sixth century CE)

*Introduction to Presocratics: A Thematic Approach to Early Greek Philosophy
with Key Readings*, First Edition. Giannis Stamatellos.
© 2012 John Wiley & Sons, Inc. Published 2012 by John Wiley & Sons, Inc.

1.1 Periods of Ancient Greek Philosophy

The Presocratic period covers the Ionians: Thales (*fl. c.* 585 BCE), Anaximander (*fl. c.* 550 BCE), Anaximenes (*fl. c.* 545 BCE), Xenophanes (*fl. c.* 540 BCE) and Heraclitus (*fl. c.* 500 BCE); Pythagoras (*fl. c.* 540 BCE) and the early Pythagoreans, for instance, Alcmaeon (*c.* 500–450 BCE) and Philolaus (*c.* 470–385 BCE); the Eleatics, namely Parmenides (*fl. c.* 480 BCE), Zeno (b. *c.* 490 BCE) and Melissus (*fl. c.* 440 BCE); and later thinkers, usually classified as 'pluralists': Empedocles (*c.* 460), Anaxagoras (*c.* 450 BCE) and the early 'atomists,' Leucippus (*fl. c.* 450 BCE) and Democritus (b. *c.* 460 BCE). Another important late Presocratic was Diogenes of Apollonia (b. *c.* 440 BCE).

The main figures of the classical period, which revolves around Athens, were Socrates (469–399 BCE), Plato (427–347 BCE) and Aristotle (384–322 BCE). Plato, the most famous follower of Socrates, established his own school, the Academy (*c.* 385 BCE), in northwest Athens; Aristotle, who was never an Athenian citizen, made extensive visits there and studied for 20 years in Plato's school before setting up one of his own, the Lyceum (*c.* 335 BCE). Other influential thinkers of the classical period were the sophists, for instance Protagoras (*fl. c.* 460 BCE) and Gorgias (b. *c.* 480 BCE), who used to tour the Greek city states as independent teachers but were especially attracted to Athens. The sophists did not constitute an organized school of thought; rather they were professional intellectuals who used to teach rhetoric, politics and philosophy for a fee. They were strongly criticized for their views by Plato and Aristotle. Plato's dialogue *The Sophist* includes a genuine critique of the sophistic movement, while Aristotle's criticism can be found in his work *Sophistical Refutations*. Plato's criticism is also expounded in dialogues such as *Protagoras* and *Gorgias*, named after famous sophists.

The Hellenistic period begins approximately after the death of Aristotle in 322 BCE and includes the following schools of philosophy:

1 The Stoic school (the "Porch," Stoa), founded by Zeno of Citium (*c.* 334–262 BCE). Cleanthes (*c.* 330–230 BCE) and Chrysippus (*c.* 280–208 BCE) were the best known scholarchs (heads) of the Old Stoa after Zeno. Stoicism survived until and throughout the imperial times, with significant thinkers such as Seneca (*c.* 1–65 BCE), Epictetus (*c.* 55–*c.* 135 CE) and Emperor Marcus Aurelius (121–180 CE).

2   The Epicurean school, known as the "Garden," founded by Epicurus
     of Samos (341–270 BCE). Metrodorus (*c.* 331–278 BCE) and Hemar-
     chus (d. 278 BCE) were eminent thinkers in Epicurus' succession.
     The Roman poet Lucretius (*c.* 90–50 BCE) was an important later
     Epicurean.
3   The Skeptic school, which had two branches: Pyrrhonian and
     Academic. The original and more radical form of Skepticism was
     established by Pyrrho of Elis (*c.* 360–270 BCE), from whom its name
     derives. Academic Skepticism was a later and milder (compromise)
     development, related to Plato's Old Academy in Athens, which went
     through a Skeptical phase and developed a probabilistic epistemol-
     ogy under the leadership of dialecticians such as Arcesilaus (*c.* 316–
     c. 241 BCE) and Carneades (214–129/8 BCE).
4   Finally, the Cynic school founded by Antisthenes of Athens (*c.* 445–
     c. 360 BCE), initially a student of Gorgias, but later a pupil and fol-
     lower of Socrates. Diogenes of Sinope (*c.* 404–*c.* 323 BCE) was a
     follower of Antisthenes and probably the most popular of the Cynics.

The late Hellenistic and Roman period, which extends far into late
antiquity, includes the philosophers and the philosophical schools that
flourished in the Roman Empire (*c.* 250 and 750 CE). During this period
there was a revival of classical philosophy, which was mainly preoccupied
with the careful study and systematic commentary of the works of
Plato and Aristotle. The most important names here are Alexander of
Aphrodisias (*fl. c.* 200 CE), Plotinus (204–270 CE), Porphyry (*c.* 232–
c. 305 CE), Iamblichus (d. *c.* 326 CE), Proclus (412–385 CE), Damascius
(*c.* 460–538 CE) and Simplicius of Cilicia (*fl. c.* 530 CE).

Damascius was the head of the Platonic Academy in Athens at the
time of its closure by the Byzantine Emperor Justinian in 529 CE.
Whereas this date is usually considered to mark the end of ancient Greek
philosophy, it should not be understood as the immediate ending of the
activities of ancient Greek thinkers. As it is reported in Agathias' *Histories*
2.30–1, Damascius and another six philosophers of the Academy, including Simplicius, migrated to Persia and joined the court of King Chosroes
I (r. 531–579 CE), in order to continue their philosophical activities.
However, they were quickly disappointed and returned to Athens, as
Agathias notes, where they enjoyed freedom from persecution after a
treaty that Chosroes concluded with Rome in 532 CE. In recent studies
it has been alternatively supported that the aforementioned philosophers
moved to Harran, where they joined a Platonic Academy that played a

significant role in the transmission of Greek philosophy to the Islamic world. The case has also been made that Simplicius, and probably other philosophers, moved to Alexandria, where Christian Neoplatonists worked systematically on commentaries to Aristotle. The school of Alexandria, as it is known today, seems to have been active until 641 CE, when the city was captured by the Muslims.

1.2   The Presocratics as Pioneers

Why did philosophy emerge in the Greek city states of Ionia in the east and in Magna Graecia (south Italy and Sicily) during the sixth century? There were a number of contributing factors, such as the early travels and explorations of the Greeks in the Mediterranean world, the special character of Greek polytheism, the emerging social structure of the *polis* and the development and promulgation of the Greek language in written texts.

Trade and travel   The Greeks of the sixth century BCE came in contact with other civilizations such as the Babylonian, the Hebrew, the Phoenician and the Egyptian. They traveled to Egypt and the Near East, engaged in trade or colonization, and, as a result, came across other customs and traditions, exchanging experiences, goods and ideas. This exchange and exploration contributed to the open-minded, pluralistic and comparative investigation of early Greek philosophy.

Religion   Ancient Greek religion was primarily a religion of cult practices, and not just a corpus of myths or a canon of sacred texts. It was an open-ended and multi-divergent narrative about the Olympian gods, without a strict or authoritative priesthood. The unrestricted character of Greek polytheism permitted to some extent divergent theoretical approaches and philosophical interpretations about the cosmos and the gods.

Language   The Greek alphabet and syntax eased the way for precision and communication in abstract and categorical thinking. Medical and mathematical treatises appeared alongside texts on geography and astronomy or the great work of Herodotus, the 'father of history.' Despite considerable dialect variations, these works became generally available, in a common and unifying Greek language, used both privately and publicly.

Society   The political and social structure was also important for early Greek philosophical inquiry and dialogue. In the sixth century BCE political movements in the Greek world generally, together with the emergence of city state democracies in particular, fostered a plurality of practices and customs and promoted critical reflection, independent argument and decision-making.

Education   Literary education in the Greek world was based on the epic poetry of Homer (the *Iliad* and the *Odyssey*) and Hesiod (roughly the *Theogony* and the *Works and Days*). Epic poetry was used as an authoritative voice to express human heroism, divine activity and the structure of the natural world. Lyric poets later turned to analyzing their conflicting emotions and, in a more private setting, raised awareness of the self. Greek education and culture encouraged questioning and a dialogue on various topics. Against this background, the Presocratics further evaluated, criticized and developed traditional worldviews and beliefs about the nature of the cosmos and of human life.

Competition   The ancient Greeks promoted the spirit of competition in such athletic events as the Isthmian, Nemean, Pythian and the Olympic games. The games included exhibitions in music and poetry, while the tragedians competed for prizes on a regular basis. The best competitors were excellent not only in physical skills, but also in intellectual abilities and talents. A spirit of intellectual competition and challenge can be found in the arguments and counter-arguments of the Presocratic thinkers.

Critical dialogue   The early Greek thinkers were in a critical, yet creative philosophical dialogue with their teachers and disciples. Anaximander challenged the cosmological views of his compatriot Thales, while Anaximander was in turn criticized by his pupil Anaximenes. Heraclitus disdained the wide learning of Pythagoras and Xenophanes; he was followed by Parmenides, who refuted Heraclitus' own theory of becoming and Ionian material monism. Zeno's paradoxes of motion and the infinite divisibility of matter were tackled in different ways by Empedocles and Democritus, while Anaxagoras' theory of mind was specifically criticized by Socrates as inadequate and disappointing.

Expression Prose became the new medium of expression for most of the Presocratics. Pherecydes of Syros seems to have been the first to compose a work in prose in a philosophical context, which was probably contemporary with Aesop's *Fables*, while in the sixth century Anaximander and Anaximenes wrote their books *On Nature* in prose, as a medium more suited to its subject matter than the elegant poetic style of Homer and Hesiod. However, some Presocratics such as Xenophanes, Parmenides and Empedocles rejected the new medium of prose and went back to the meter and style of earlier formal poetry, adapting it to their ways of thinking.

1.3 Presocratic Historiography

The adjective 'Presocratic' (*Vorsokratiker* in German) is a term introduced by German scholars of the nineteenth and early twentieth century to denote, historically and philosophically, the period before Socrates (469–399 BCE). Whereas from a historical perspective the term 'Presocratics' identifies those thinkers who lived before the time of Socrates, from a philosophical perspective the Presocratic tradition contains a lot more than the 'naturalistic tradition' that precedes the anthropocentric spirit of Socrates' ethical teaching. Earlier ethical inquiries can be found in Xenophanes, Heraclitus, Empedocles and the Pythagoreans. Moreover, Presocratic thinkers did not all have the same philosophical views. For instance, Parmenides' theory of being contrasts Heraclitus' theory of becoming, while the materialism of the early atomists is quite different from the material monism of the Milesian thinkers. Thus it could be suggested that the phrase 'early Greek philosophers' might be more appropriate in the light of these philosophers' intellectual innovation.

In modern Presocratic scholarship two tendencies can be identified: (1) the historico-philosophical approach, which begins with such German scholars as Zeller, Nestle, Diels and Kranz; and (2) the analytical approach, which includes British and American scholars such as Burnet, Cornford, Cherniss, Dodds, Vlastos, Owen and Barnes. The former is an approach in the continental tradition, incorporating elements of Hegelian dialectical historicism and phenomenology; the latter follows a line of philosophical argumentation and formal logic inaugurated by G. E. Moore, Bertrand Russell and Ludwig Wittgenstein. However, it has to be noted that in recent Presocratic studies these two tendencies have merged into a project of historical, philosophical and anthropological exploration of early Greek philosophical tradition.

Modern interest in early Greek philosophy can be traced back to 1573, when Henri Estienne (better known under his Latinized name Stephanus) collected a number of Presocratic fragments in *Poesis philosophica*. In the eighteenth and early nineteenth century there were available editions on Empedocles and Parmenides. In the early nineteenth century Simon Karsten edited the three philosophers who wrote in verse: Xenophanes, Parmenides and Empedocles. In 1838 Ritter and Preller published the first edition of *Historia philosophiae Graecae* (the tenth and last edition appeared in 1934), which included the Presocratics.

Eduard Zeller was the first scholar to study the Presocratics systematically, which he did in his massive and influential history of Greek philosophy *Die Philosophie der Griechen* (1844–1852). His exposition followed a historical classification, reflected in its division into three volumes. Volume 1 dealt with the Presocratics, from Thales to the sophists (*Vorsokratische Philosophie*); volume 2 was devoted to philosophers of the classical period, from Socrates to Aristotle; and volume 3 embraced the entire Hellenistic period and beyond, going from the early third century BCE until late antiquity (sixth century CE). Zeller's book went through many editions.

In 1879 the German scholar and classicist Hermann Diels published another monumental and hugely influential book: *Doxographi Graeci*, a collection of those ancient sources that included summaries of the views of early Greek thinkers; such views are found particularly in authors of the Hellenistic and Roman period (like Plutarch or Galen) and of late antiquity in general, but also in mainstream classical philosophers (like Plato and Aristotle). Diels is also the one who coined the term "doxography" from the Greek *doxa* ("opinion," "view"). His research focused on topics concerning physics and metaphysics – theology, cosmology, astronomy, meteorology, biology – but not on ethics. In 1883, F. W. A. Müllach edited the *Fragmenta philosophorum Graecorum*, which included a number of Presocratic fragments with a Latin translation and, occasionally, a short commentary. In 1887 Paul Tannery, in his book *Pour l'Histoire de la science hellène*, set the Presocratics in a scientific framework. The first English "textbook" on the Presocratics, *Early Greek Philosophy*, had been published only five years before, in 1892. It was written by the famous Scottish scholar John Burnet. The first complete edition of the Presocratics, however – Diels' monumental *Die Fragmente der Vorsokratiker* – appeared only in 1903. In 1934 Diels's pupil Walhter

Kranz prepared a fifth edition of it, and in 1951 he published the sixth and final edition, which included revisions and corrections in the form of supplementary notes in each of the three volumes. This Diels–Kranz (DK) edition of 1951 became the standard reference work in the field of Presocratic scholarship.

THE PHILOSOPHERS

Introduction

Presocratic philosophy began in the Greek city states of Ionia, moved to south Italy and Sicily, and ended in Athens and Thrace. Miletus was the native city of Thales, Anaximander and Anaximenes; Colophon, that of Xenophanes; Ephesus, that of Heraclitus; Samos, that of Pythagoras and Melissus; Elea, that of Parmenides and Zeno; Acragas in Sicily, that of Empedocles; Clazomenae, that of Anaxagoras; Abdera, that of Leucippus and Democritus. Anaxagoras and Democritus went to Athens and possibly met Socrates there.

Introduction to Presocratics: A Thematic Approach to Early Greek Philosophy with Key Readings, First Edition. Giannis Stamatellos.
© 2012 John Wiley & Sons, Inc. Published 2012 by John Wiley & Sons, Inc.

2.1   A Precursor: Pherecydes of Syros

Pherecydes of Syros (born c. 600 BCE) should be considered as an important forerunner of Presocratic thought. He seems to be the first thinker who attempted a proto-cosmological explanation of the creation myth. At *Metaphysics* 1091^b, Aristotle states that Pherecydes is a philosopher who "blends" the mythical with the non-mythical. In *Heptamychia* – probably the first work in prose in Greek literature – Pherecydes claimed that, at the beginning of the cosmos, three primary, everlasting and self-creative principles existed: Zeus, Chronos ("Time") and Chthonie (the Ionic form of the feminine Chthonia, "Earth") (B1).

2.2   The Ionians

Thales of Miletus (*fl. c.* 585 BCE) is regarded as the founder of Western philosophy. He was the first thinker who tried to explain nature in a non-mythical discourse by introducing **material monism** as an explanation of the cosmos. He is also regarded as the sage who introduced the Delphic saying "know thyself" (A1 and A2). Whereas Thales was an admired figure in antiquity, only a few testimonies survive concerning his life and work. Some ancient authors ascribe to him the work *Nautical Star Guide*,

> **material monism**
>
> the theory that everything originates from a single basic material stuff

while, according to some others, he wrote two more works: *On the Solstice* and *On the Equinox* (A1). Thales was an avid traveler and Herodotus provides important evidence for his activities as statesman and engineer (A6). He was also a mathematician and geometer and, as Heraclitus testifies, the first who worked on astronomical problems (B38). According to later testimonies, Thales would have foretold the eclipse of the sun in 585 BCE (A2); diverted the river Halys, so that Croesus' army could cross it (A6); and measured the pyramids of Egypt by using their shadow (A1, A21). As a mathematician, Thales is acknowledged by Proclus (following Eudemus) as the discoverer of a number of theorems (A20).

Anaximander (*fl. c.* 550 BCE) was a pupil of Thales. He studied the natural phenomena and made the first comprehensive attempt to explain the origins both of animal species and of the cosmos as a whole. He thought that the first living organisms were generated from moisture that the sun caused to evaporate, while humans were born from a fish-like

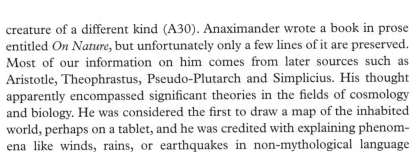

creature of a different kind (A30). Anaximander wrote a book in prose entitled *On Nature*, but unfortunately only a few lines of it are preserved. Most of our information on him comes from later sources such as Aristotle, Theophrastus, Pseudo-Plutarch and Simplicius. His thought apparently encompassed significant theories in the fields of cosmology and biology. He was considered the first to draw a map of the inhabited world, perhaps on a tablet, and he was credited with explaining phenomena like winds, rains, or earthquakes in non-mythological language (A1, A6).

Anaximenes (*fl. c.* 545 BCE) was a pupil of Anaximander. He is the third and the last of the Milesian philosophers. Only a few sources concerning his life and activities survive. He wrote a book in prose, probably within the same framework of natural philosophy as that of Anaximander, but in 'simple' language, as the report goes (A1). Anaximenes was interested in cosmology and meteorology, and some of his ideas in these areas survive. His natural philosophy influenced some later Presocratics, Diogenes of Apollonia in particular (*fl. c.* 410–322 BCE).

Aristotle said that Xenophanes (*fl. c.* 540 BCE) was the first "who looked up at the sky and had a theory of everything" (*Metaphysics* 986ᵇ). Xenophanes was born in Colophon, an Ionian Greek city of Asia Minor, but he emigrated to the West – to Sicily or southern Italy (A1). For this reason he was probably related to the Pythagoreans and the Eleatics, even though there is no significant evidence in support of this view (A29). Xenophanes seems to have lived a long life; in his own words, "already there are seven and sixty years tossing my thought up and down the land of Greece; and from my birth there were another twenty-five to add to these . . ." (A1).

Xenophanes introduced a new kind of philosophical poetry, which could be regarded as a response to the philosophical prose of the Milesians. In particular, he wrote didactic poetry in epic meter, elegiacs and iambics; and he also wrote satirical poems in hexameter, known as *Silloi*. Xenophanes criticized Homer and Hesiod for the immorality of their myths (B12). In the extant lines of his work one can observe philosophical inquiries on ethics, divinity and the physical structure of the cosmos.

Heraclitus (*fl. c.* 500 BCE) was born in Ephesus. He wrote a single book with the title *On Nature* (A1). Heraclitus dedicated and placed his book in the temple of Artemis, as a city treasure to be safeguarded. In the surviving fragments of his work we can appreciate a man of strong and independent philosophical spirit, who speculated on physics, ethics and politics. However, Heraclitus was known in antiquity as "the obscure philosopher," on account of the ambiguity of his thought and enigmatic character of his language. His book was obscure on purpose, so that only those of rank and influence may have access to it. This explains Socrates' alleged statement about Heraclitus' book: "the concepts I understand are great, but I believe that the concepts I can't understand are great, too. However, the reader needs to be an excellent diver, like those from Delos, to get to the bottom of it" (Diogenes Laertius, *Lives of the Philosophers* 2.22).

2.3   The Pythagoreans

Pythagoras (*fl. c.* 540 BCE) was born on the island of Samos and traveled, it was said, for many years in Egypt and the orient, being influenced by oriental thought. Driven out by Samos' tyrannical rule, Pythagoras migrated to south Italy around 532 BCE. He established in Croton a school of his own, which had both philosophical and political aims. Pythagoras is one of the most enigmatic figures of antiquity. Much of the information we have on his life and activities is dubious and comes from two very late biographies (or rather hagiographies): Porphyry's *Vita Pythagorae* and Iamblichus' *De vita Pythagorica*. According to these Neoplatonic sources, Pythagoras' students were divided into two groups: those who had permission only to attend and 'listen to' his lectures – the *akousmatikoi* – and those who could participate in the inner-circle 'lessons' of the school – the *mathematikoi*.

Pythagoras is acknowledged as an important mathematician, and it is generally assumed that he has proved the incommensurability between the side and the diagonal of a square and the equivalence between the square of the hypotenuse and the sum of the squares of the sides in a right-angled triangle (which is known today as Pythagoras' theorem) (Diogenes Laertius, *Lives of the Philosophers* 8.12). According to Diogenes Laertius (A1), he was the first to introduced the term *philosophia* ("love of wisdom") and the first to call himself a *philosophos*. Pythagoras wrote nothing; it is alleged that he preferred to have his teachings recorded in the minds of his disciples (Plutarch, *Numa* 22). The exact details of his teaching remain vague, due to the "silence" of his associates (Porphyry, *Vita Pythagorae* 19). However, some of his doctrines probably survive in the writings of later Pythagorean thinkers such as Alcmaeon of Croton (*c.* 500–450 BCE) and Philolaus of Croton (*c.* 470–385 BCE).

It is noteworthy that the Pythagoreans brought a radical change to the explanation of the cosmos and of the nature of the soul. They followed a disciplined life of practical rules and prohibitions; they shared their possessions, meals, readings and exercises; and they placed a special focus on the study of mathematics, music and philosophy, which were used both for educative and for therapeutic reasons. Pythagorean harmonics is particularly related to the structure of the universe as well as to the sacred symbol of the **tetractus**. According to Iamblichus, Pythagoras regarded the *tetractus* as the key to understanding the universe; the cause and root of everything, the "fount of ever-flowing nature" (*De vita Pythagorica* 29.162).

> ### *tetractus*
> the first four numbers, which, together, add up to 10; number 10 is the "whole of number" — the perfect number that contains all music ratios, and it can be arranged geometrically, to form a perfect equilateral triangle of four units on each side

2.4 The Eleatics

Parmenides (*fl. c.* 480 BCE) was in the second generation of Greeks who had settled in the colony of Elea in southern Italy, and so his philosophy was known as 'Eleatic'. Diogenes Laertius describes Parmenides as a disciple of Aminias the Pythagorean (A1). In spite of the limited information that survives about his life, Parmenides was one of the most important Presocratic figures, and one especially favored by Plato and, later, by the Platonists. For instance, Plato calls Parmenides 'great' in the *Sophist* (237a4–5), and in the *Theaetetus* (183e ff.) he describes him as 'revered' and 'awe-inspiring'. It is also notable that Plato makes him the instructor and critic of the young Socrates and the central figure of the dialogue *Parmenides*, a work with a significant place and function in Plato's own development and a strong impact on the Platonic tradition.

Parmenides composed a poem entitled *On Nature*, which was written in the traditional form of the Homeric hexameter. The poem is divided into three parts: (1) the prologue; (2) the Way of Truth (*alētheia*); and (3) the Way of Opinion (*doxa*). In the prologue, which is preserved by Simplicius in its entirety, Parmenides describes a spiritual journey taken by a 'young man' (*kouros*) to an unnamed goddess. The young man (probably Parmenides himself) is driven in a flying chariot by the daughters of Helios, following the sun's path, to an unnamed goddess who reveals to him the two possible ways of inquiry: the unshaken heart of truth and the doubtful opinions of mortals (B1). The style of the prologue is allegorical and autobiographical, reflecting probably some Orphic or oriental influences. It is worth mentioning that the image of the chariot is later found in Plato's *Phaedrus* in the myth of the soul, as well as being a standard metaphor for poetic inspiration. Then, in the Way of Truth, the goddess reveals the truth about reality, while in the Way of Opinion she develops a false account of reality, which is compatible with, or reproduces, human opinion.

In his poem Parmenides aims at justifying the unique and unconditional existence of being through the rational refutation of not-being. His method is to make 'what-is,' taken at the simplest and most basic level, into a subject of speech and thought; then he deduces the characteristics of eternity, changelessness and immobility from this basic premise, by a chain of irrefutable arguments.

Zeno of Elea (*fl. c.* 450 BCE) was a disciple of Parmenides. Plato's character Socrates addresses him as the 'Eleatic Palamedes' in the *Sophist* (216a) and *Phaedrus* (261d) and makes him his main interlocutor in the *Parmenides*, in the setting of which Zeno is presented as visiting Athens along with his master Parmenides, for a lecture at the Ceramicus. Plato shows Zeno expounding a series of rigorous arguments in support of Parmenides' philosophy as a model for training in philosophy. Moreover, Aristotle attributes to Zeno the invention of dialectic (A10). According to other testimonies (A1, A2, A6–A9), Zeno is characterized as a noble figure, both as a philosopher and as a politician. In all probability he participated in a plot to overthrow the tyrant of Elea and showed considerable courage during his torture and execution (A1).

Zeno wrote a book in prose to support Parmenides' theory of a changeless, unique and unqualified being. Its aim was to demonstrate the absurd consequences of rejecting Eleatic theory; and he did this through a collection of mathematical puzzles, paradoxes and dilemmas. The kernel of Zeno's argument consists of two refutations: the denial of plurality and the denial of motion. Zeno's refutations are expressed through a series of logical **antinomies**, which survive in Simplicius' commentary on Aristotle's *Physics*, as well as through the details of four famous puzzles, which involve a series of paradoxes about perceptible reality, physical motion, time and

antinomy

the contradictory conclusion that arises from two hypothetical syllogisms, each of which appears to be independently true, but cannot be true simultaneously with the other

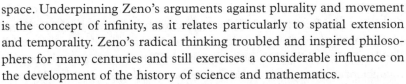

space. Underpinning Zeno's arguments against plurality and movement is the concept of infinity, as it relates particularly to spatial extension and temporality. Zeno's radical thinking troubled and inspired philosophers for many centuries and still exercises a considerable influence on the development of the history of science and mathematics.

Melissus of Samos (*fl. c.* 440 BCE) is the third important Eleatic philosopher, after Parmenides and Zeno. Melissus was also a naval commander famous for his victories, especially the one against the Athenian fleet, in 441 BCE (A3). He probably wrote one philosophical book in prose, probably entitled *On Nature* or *On What Exists*, from which only ten fragments survive – again, preserved by Simplicius – although some there are some paraphrases of Melissus in the pseudo-Aristotelian treatise *On Melissus, Xenophanes and Gorgias* (A5). Melissus' argument reflects Parmenides' line of reasoning in the Way of Truth; it follows the main principles of Parmenides' thought, but not all its details. Whereas Melissus agrees with Parmenides' conclusions on the indestructibility, immobility, indivisibility, oneness, completeness, changelessness and perfection of being, he develops a different view on its timelessness and infinity.

2.5 The Pluralists

In response to the arguments of the Eleatics, later Presocratics devised various ways of reintroducing plurality and change into the natural world in minimal ways. The cosmos, for them, was not determined by a single corporeal or incorporeal principle, but through the synthesis and divergence of many principles and powers. It is not the plurality of things that derives from one single principle (one → many), but the plurality of principles that determine the unity of the cosmos (many → one) and the diversity of physical phenomena (many → many). The main philosophers who followed this "pluralistic" direction (the so-called "pluralists" or Neo-Ionians) were Empedocles, Anaxagoras and the atomists – Leucippus and Democritus.

Empedocles (*c.* 460 BCE) flourished in the city of Acragas, Sicily. He was an exuberant and influential figure, taking part vigorously in the political and social activities of his city; he stands for the ancient *persona* of the wise man who leads his fellow citizens with his political actions and judicious words. He seems to have been in favor of democracy, an opponent of aristocracy and oligarchy; he also had a reputation as a healer. Various stories about his life survive in antiquity, some probably fictitious. The best known is the legend of his death, which describes him jumping into the volcanic crater of Mount Etna to convince his pupils of his divinity. His philosophical brilliance was not only praised by ancient authors such as Lucretius, but is also reflected by the great influence he exercised on other philosophical traditions, such as Islamic Neoplatonism, Renaissance literature and romanticism.

Like Xenophanes and Parmenides, Empedocles wrote poetry in the form of the Homeric hexameter. His poetry reflects didactic and rhetorical skills, and for this reason Aristotle regards Empedocles as the inventor of rhetoric (A86). Empedocles wondered at the nature and structure of the physical world. He seems to be also influenced to some extent by Pythagorean and Orphic doctrines of the soul. A considerable number of fragments survive from Empedocles' poems. In 1990 an ancient papyrus with some of Empedocles' fragments was found at the University of Strasbourg; this papyrus, published in 1999, is known as the Strasbourg papyrus.

Anaxagoras (c. 450 BCE) was born in the Ionian city of Clazomenae and he was the first Presocratic philosopher to live and teach in Athens. He wrote only one book in prose (A1, A37), on natural philosophy with reference to astronomical and meteorological phenomena. It was available in the Athenian *agora* and, according to Socrates (Plato, *Apology* 26d), it could be purchased for "a drachma, at most." Unfortunately only a small number of fragments survive from Anaxagoras' book, preserved mainly in the work of later thinkers such as Plutarch, Sextus and Simplicius. The content of Anaxagoras' extant fragments show an original thinker who inquired on the generation of the cosmos, the structure of the physical universe and the nature of human knowledge.

Anaxagoras was famous for his theory of mind, a theory so famous in antiquity that he received the nickname *nous*, since this is the word he used for "mind" (A2, A15 and A24). Anaxagoras was also the first philosopher in Athens to be brought to trial for impiety (c. 433 BCE). According to ancient sources, he was exiled from the city and spent the rest of his life in Lampsacus of Ionia; presumably this was the result of the influential intervention of his student and friend, Pericles, who saved his teacher from death (A1, A3, A15 and A17). Anaxagoras' association with Pericles was probably the motive for his trial in the first place, although the philosopher was formally accused on account of his materialistic theories, and in particular his atheistic view that the celestial bodies – the sun, the moon and the stars – were not gods but fiery masses of red-hot stones (A1–A3, A19). Anaxagoras may have envisioned this theory due to a meteorite that fell on earth at Aigospotamoi, in Thrace, around 467 BCE (A11–A12).

Leucippus (*fl. c.* 450 BCE) and Democritus (born *c.* 460 BCE) are often taken together as the proponents of **atomic theory**. They are usually classified as early atomists, in contrast with later exponents of this theory; for atomism was developed Hellenistic philosophy in Epicurus' school, the Garden. Leucippus and Democritus were from Abdera in Thrace – the birthplace of the sophist Protagoras, who was reported (A9) to have been a pupil of Democritus or associated with him in some way. Democritus acquired the nickname "Laugher," apparently because he used to laugh at anyone who would not recognize the truth behind the conventional reality (A16 and A20).

> **atomic theory**
>
> the view that everything consists of imperceptible and indivisible units of matter, called atoms: the atoms and the void are the principles of everything

His humorous attitude towards his fellow citizens is usually contrasted with Heraclitus' misanthropic pessimism. Democritus visited Athens and may have met Socrates there, but he was disappointed to find that no one had heard of him (B116): "I came to Athens and no one knew me."

Leucippus wrote only one book, *On Mind*, but Democritus was a prolific author. Diogenes Laertius called Democritus a *pentathlos* in philosophy (that is, a victor in the context of the five main forms of combat in the games): he had works on physics, theology, epistemology, psychology and ethics (A1). Democritus' most significant books were the *Great World-System*, *On the Nature of the World* and the *Lesser World-System* (A1–A2). The last title is also attributed to Leucippus.

Democritus was devoted to philosophical inquiry. He used to say that he would rather discover a single explanation related to the cosmos than acquire the kingdom of the Persians (B118). It is worth mentioning that he seems to be in contact with Hindu and oriental philosophy (A1), and it is striking that, in the sixth century BCE, the Hindu philosopher Kanada developed a theory of atoms. However, Kanada's theory has a teleological slant not observed in the extant fragments of Democritus – and it is noteworthy that in Greek philosophy as a whole atomism and teleology go in opposite directions. Unfortunately, little survives of Democritus' atomism in his own words; most of the extant fragments from his works are on ethics.

Finally, another important figure among the early atomists was Metrodorus of Chios (*fl. c.* 400 BCE). He approved of Democritus' atomic theory but combined it with an extreme form of negative skepticism: "we know nothing, no, not even whether we know or not" (B1). Metrodorus was influential on Hellenistic philosophy – both on Epicurus' relativism and on Pyrrho's skepticism.

Conclusion

The first Presocratic philosophers flourished in the Mediterranean world of the sixth and the fifth century BCE, mainly along the Ionian coast of Asia Minor, and then in the western part of the Greek world (Graecia Magna). Thales, Anaximander and Anaximenes were natives of Miletus, Xenophanes of Colophon and Heraclitus of Ephesus. They were followed by the Pythagoreans and the Eleatics in south Italy; these practiced philosophy in Croton and Elea respectively. The next influential figure, Empedocles, came from Acragas in Sicily. With Leucippus and Democritus we move to Abdera in northern Greece; and, finally, Anaxagoras of Clazomenae, another Ionian, brought the interests of Presocratic philosophy to Athens. With respect to their philosophical theories, the Presocratics are usually classified as Ionians, Pythagoreans, Eleatics and pluralists (or Neo-Ionians). Their philosophical work is typically found in one single book per philosopher; such books are composed in prose or in verse and they treat various topics, in particular from natural philosophy, cosmology and the study of being.

PRINCIPLES

Introduction

The Presocratics inquired into the primary principles of the cosmos and of being. The Ionians argued for the existence of a primary physical stuff of the universe, which is known to us as the *archē* of all things. In contrast to this physical *archē*, the Pythagoreans introduced an incorporeal formal principle, namely number (*arithmos*). Later Presocratics supported a plurality of principles, including matter and forces, on which, in their view, the world would be founded.

> **archē**
>
> beginning; first or primary principle (here, in ontology)

Introduction to Presocratics: A Thematic Approach to Early Greek Philosophy with Key Readings, First Edition. Giannis Stamatellos.
© 2012 John Wiley & Sons, Inc. Published 2012 by John Wiley & Sons, Inc.

3.1   Material Explanations

Thales seems to be the first thinker who speculated about the existence of a single material stuff with a primordial role in the composition of the universe, claiming that the fundamental principle of all natural phenomena is water (*hudōr*). As Aristotle testifies at *Metaphysics* 983^b (A12):

> There always has to be some natural substance, one or more than one, which endures while the rest are generated from it. They do not however all agree on the number and character of such a principle. Thales, the founder of this type of philosophy, says that the first principle is water (and that is why he claimed that the earth rests on water), perhaps having reached this conclusion from observing that nourishment is universally moist, and that even heat is generated from moisture and fuelled by it [...] That is why he reached this conclusion, and also because seed generally has a moist character and water is the principle of what has the natural character of being moist.

Along with the reasons suggested by Aristotle in A12, it may well be that the vital importance of water in nature as along with human-dependent considerations about the value of water in the creation of social and economic wealth contributed to Thales' conclusion. Thales seems also to follow the traditional Homeric world-image where the cosmic river Oceanos, which surrounds the surface of the earth, is the source of all mortal and immortal life (*Iliad* 14.244, 201, 302). Moreover, Thales' theory of water as the *archē* of all things lends itself to two possible interpretations: (1) the material principle interpretation, according to which everything is *made of* water; and (2) the originative principle interpretation, which states that water is *the source* of everything. Whereas the first interpretation seems to be followed by Aristotle in the passage quoted above (A12), the second interpretation could lead us to the conclusion that water is the originative source of everything even though not everything is made of water. Both interpratations underlie the importance of Thales' novelty in the explanation of physical reality through a single material principle.

The two other Milesians, Anaximander and Anaximenes, differentiated their views from those of Thales. Whereas the latter identified the primary principle with a particular and definite stuff, Anaximander argued for an unlimited and indefinite material mass, which he called the *apeiron* (A9–A11). Like Hesiod's primordial **chaos**, Anaximander's *apeiron* is the neutral source from which all things derive. All things arise in a cyclical process of coming-to-be and passing-away (B1):

> **chaos**
>
> featureless pre-cosmic abyss; the source of everything according to Hesiod

> From the source from which they arise, to that they return of necessity when they are destroyed, "for they suffer punishment and make reparation to one another for their injustice according to the assessment of time," as he [Anaximander] says in somewhat poetical terms.

Anaximander's *apeiron* is the eternal originative material mass, *without limits* in time, space, quality and quantity. It is without temporal limits because it is everlasting, unborn, ageless, deathless and indestructible (A15 and B3); without spatial limits because it has no restrictions in space (A15); without quantitative limits because it is inexhaustible in its mass (A14); and without any particular quality because it is indefinite: perceptible qualities such as 'hot' and 'cold' are opposite forces that arise from its neutrality and limitless nature (A16).

Anaximenes maintained that the source of all things is not an indefinite and unlimited *apeiron* but *air* (*aēr*): a definite but *infinite* material stuff. The air is the source of life that encloses the cosmos and the first principle responsible for the maintenance of all living organisms (B2). Everything is produced through quantitative differences of the air (A5–A7): through a process of 'rarefaction,' air becomes fire, and through a process of 'condensation' it becomes water and then earth (B1): 'hot' and 'cold' are dispositions of matter that supervene on changes. Anaximenes illustrates his view with the process of breathing: "for the breath is chilled by being compressed and condensed with the lips, but when the mouth is loosened the breath escapes and becomes warm through its rarity" (B1).

Xenophanes of Colophon seems to have been influenced by Ionian physicalism. He considered earth (*gaia*) and water (*hudōr*) to be the basic material principles or stuffs of all beings (B29 and B33). According to him, all living beings are composed of earth and water (B29: "everything that is born and growing is earth and water"), and human beings are generated the same way (B33: "we all are generated from earth and water"). Xenophanes attached particular importance to earth in the cosmic cycle: "for all things are from earth and into earth all things come to their end" (B27). Moreover, he describes, in non-mythical terms, the material causalities that generate and elucidate natural phenomena – for example, the sea is the primary cause of clouds, winds, rain and rivers (B30): "the sea is the source of water and the source of wind; for without the great sea there would be <no wind> nor flowing rivers nor rain from the sky, but the great sea is the father of clouds and winds and rivers."

Heraclitus of Ephesus conceived of the natural world as resulting from the alterations of a single material principle: fire (*pur*). Fire is the *archē* of all things (B31) and the basic material stuff of cosmic exchange, in the same way as gold, which is traded but sets the standard of the exchange (B90): "all things are an equal exchange for fire and fire for all things, as goods are for gold and gold for goods." Fire preserves the unity of the universe within an everlasting cosmic cycle of alterations (B31). Heraclitus also recognized an internal hidden rhythm of nature, which is responsible for the movement and regulation of all things, namely the *logos* (B1):

> Of the *logos*, which is as I describe it, people always prove to be uncomprehending both before they have heard it and once they have heard it. For, although all things happen according to the logos, people are like those of no experience, even when they do experience such words and deeds as I explain when I distinguish each thing according to its **phusis** and declare how it is; but others fail to notice what they do after they wake up just as they forget what they do when asleep.

> **phusis**
>
> natural constitution and development of things

Logos is the one guiding principle of all things, which includes in itself perfectly, controls, and unifies two opposite tensions, and the resulting unitary pattern is realized through the conjunction of opposite pairs: "as the same thing there exist in us living and dead, waking and sleeping, young and old; for these change round and are those, and those change round and are these" (B88).

For Heraclitus, natural phenomena are external indications of a complex cosmic network of fire and *logos* wherein the unity of *logos* establishes the ontological connection between the apparent pluralities and oppositions generated by fire. Nature "loves to hide" (B123) in an unseen harmony and unity (B50 and B54). Harmony derives from opposite tensions and conflicts (B51 B54), as it is expressed through the image of 'war' (B53): "War is father of all and king of all: some he shows as gods, others as men; some he makes slaves, others free." From opposition comes conjunction, and from tones that are at variance comes the perfect harmony (B8). Plurality derives from unity and unity emerges from plurality (B10: "combinations: wholes and not wholes, being like and being different, in tune and out of tune, and from all things one, and from one all things"). Thus, despite apparent multiplicity in the cosmos, all things are one and unified in their totality (B50).

Diogenes of Apollonia developed and reaffirmed Ionian material monism (B2). His argument is that all things are modifications of one basic *archē* – not because it is simple and unique per se, but as a consequence of the impossibility of interaction between distinct opposite substances. He maintained that the *archē* of the universe is an *in-between* stuff, made of *air* and *fire:* an infinite and eternal material principle that, through condensation and rarefaction – like the air of Anaximenes – causes all things to come into being and pass away (A5).

3.2   Formal Principles

Pythagoras explained perceptible reality not in terms of material causality but on the basis of mathematical relations and structures. The Pythagoreans defined material beings through non-material entities – numbers – and the structure of the perceptible universe through imperceptible mathematical connections. Number is the eternal principle that animates all things. The power of number is realized and expressed in the cosmos, in the soul and in all being. The Pythagoreans analyzed the physical world according to a structure of discrete interconnected mathematical units and, as Aristotle explained, they regarded number as the first principle both of physical objects themselves and of their properties and states (*Metaphysics* 986^a).

The Pythagorean first principle is therefore not water, air or fire but a divine *number*: the One or the Monad (Philolaus B8: "the one is the first principle of all things"). The Monad is not the first in a series of number – it is not even a number itself – but the generator of numbers, the 'principle' or 'origin' of all numbers. The Pythagoreans embellished numbers and figures with appellations related to the gods. According to Plutarch (*De Iside et Osiride* 354F2–3 and 381E9–F3), the Monad was identified with Apollo, the sun god, and it is noteworthy that Pythagoras himself had the name 'Hyperborean Apollo' (Aelian, *Varia historia* 2.26 and Iamblichus, *De vita Pythagorica* 91, 135, 140). The Pythagoreans also identified the Monad with the *hearth fire* at the centre of the universe (Aristotle, *Metaphysics* 986^a).

In the Pythagorean 'table of opposites,' reported by Aristotle at *Metaphysics* 986ª22, there are ten pairs of opposites where the first column signifies the positive side of the opposition, while the second column the negative side:

Limit	Unlimited
Odd	Even
One	Plurality
Right	Left
Male	Female
Resting	Moving
Straight	Curved
Light	Darkness
Good	Bad
Square	Oblong

According to Aristotle, the Pythagorean thinker who introduced the table of opposites was the philosopher and physician Alcmaeon of Croton. As a physician, Alcmaeon believed that health consists in the equilibrium of the body's component contraries. For this reasons he explained that ***isonomia*** – the state of balance – between opposite powers such as wet/dry, cold/hot, bitter/sweet maintains health, but ***monarchia*** – that is, absolute rule – of one of them over the others produces disease (B4). It was the task of the physician to restore the balance and heal the patient.

> **isonomia**
>
> equality of opposite powers

> **monarchia**
>
> monarchy; rule by one power

The Pythagorean Philolaus of Croton developed still further the importance of numerical groupings and the divine properties of number. For him, number has three kinds: (1) the odd; (2) the even; and (3) the even–odd (B5); and all things are manifestations of these number-forms in various physical representations. Philolaus explained the harmony of the universe as being due to the mathematical relation between numbers, expressed in the ordered cosmos (B2): "what limits and what is unlimited together make a harmony of the *kosmos* and the things in it."

3.3   One and Many

In Sicily, Empedocles of Acragas (another *polis* of Magna Graecia) returned to Ionian physicalism and developed an aspect of it that is usually regarded as an incipient version of **hylozoism**. However, he opened an alternative to the 'single' *archē* of his predecessors by suggesting a plurality of principles: firstly, the immortal, unchangeable and imperishable four elements – fire, air, water and earth – and, secondly, the two eternal and opposite forces of Love and Strife. Whereas the *four roots* are indestructible, imperishable and immortal corporeal or physical elements, Love and Strife are

> **hylozoism**
>
> the theory that matter includes a self-developing living force that can produce and reproduce the living organism, usually without external intervention

the two opposite forces of attraction and repulsion in the cosmos that act upon the four 'roots.' The metaphor of 'roots' (*rhizomata*) for the elements indicates the vitality of the substructure, its unseen depths and the potentiality for growth (B6): "Hear first the four roots of all things: bright Zeus and life-bringing Hera and Aidoneus and Nestis, whose tears are the source of mortal streams." In this fragment Zeus corresponds to fire, Hera to air, Nestis to water and Aidoneus to earth. The four Empedoclean elements are defined as the immortal material principles that make up the countless types of mortals beings, by 'running through each other' while they themselves remain fundamentally unaltered and imperishable (B35); they are without birth or death (B7), the only real things (B21), equal, indestructible, always the same, alike in age, while each has its particular prerogatives and properties (B17).

For Empedocles, everything is a mixing and a separating of the 'roots,' which in this way appear in the guise of various kinds of mortal things. Since nothing comes to be or passes away in the strict sense, there is no generation or destruction. Generation is to be explained as the *mixture* of the elements in various proportions through the act of Love, while destruction is the *separation* of the various compounds into their original elements through the act of Strife (B8 and B21). Empedocles uses the simile of the artist who produces all the figures and objects in his painting through the combination of a few basic colors (B23):

> As painters, men well taught by wisdom in the practice of their art, decorate temple offerings–they take in their hands pigments of various colours,

and after fitting them in close combination, more of some and less of others, they produce from them shapes resembling all things, creating trees and men and women, animals and birds and water-nourished fish, and long-lived gods too, highest in honour; so do not let your mind be deceived into thinking that there is any other source for the countless perishables that are seen, but know this clearly, since the discourse you have heard is from a god.

Love and Strife, in a sense, both generate and destroy. However, the completeness of the four elements establishes the continuity of being, so that there are no spatial gaps: "there is no part of the whole that is empty" (B13).

Following Empedocles, Anaxagoras maintained that coming to be and passing away are internal cosmic processes of mixing and separation – coming to be is the mixture of stuffs and passing away the separation of stuffs (B17):

> The Greeks are not right to think that there is generation and destruction, for nothing is generated or destroyed, but there is a mixing and a separating of existing things. And so they would be right to call generation mixing and destruction separating.

Like Empedocles, and in contrast to his Ionian predecessors, Anaxagoras introduced more than a single *archē*. He supported two cosmic principles, which were infinite and everlasting in nature: the original mixture of a pre-cosmic matter, where everything remained potentially in a compact form of elemental *ingredients*; and *nous* (mind), an active and formative force, which initiated the separation of the ingredients and created an ever expanding universe through an encircling motion – a vortex.

For Anaxagoras, the original mixture is an all-inclusive pre-cosmic matter of homogenous parts; and these are the *ingredients* (B1–B4). The ingredients of the original mixture are an infinite number of 'seeds' – for example opposites like dry, hot and cold, bright and dark. However, opposites are not substances, they are qualities that embody substances. The 'seeds' are neither generated nor destroyed; they are the indivisible and imperishable components of homogenous parts, unlimited in number, shape, color and taste, each part containing portions of everything. The seeds are not just a collection of opposites, but also what we may regard as the biological constituents of things that are essential to the development of an organism: "the milk of the bird is the white of the egg" (B20).

Anaxagoras' *nous* is completely separate from matter, and this is the only exception to the universal principle that 'everything is in everything' (B11): "In everything there is a portion of everything except of mind (*nous*), but some have mind as well." *Nous* is described as 'unlimited,' 'self-controlling,' 'unmixed,' 'alone in itself and by itself,' 'the finest,' 'the purest,' 'possessing complete knowledge,' 'supreme in power,' 'the controller of every living thing' (B12). *Nous* is the active maker of the cosmos (A48); it is the beginning of motion and time (A64); a supreme, divine, self-controlling, everlasting and unlimited principle, which initiates the original rotation of matter, controls the consequent separations and arranges the whole in an ordered cosmos (B1–B2).

Anaxagoras denied void and limit in the division of corporeal bodies (A44 and A68). The original mixture is infinitely reducible in smallness and infinitely expandable in largeness (B3):

> There is no least of what is small, but always a lesser (for it is not possible for what there is not to be); and there is always a larger than the large, and equal to the small in amount; for each thing in relation to itself is both large and small.

Whereas the nature of all things is infinite in size and quantity at a universal level – there being no 'least' of what is small, and always a 'larger' than the large – limitation is found when each thing is compared to itself at a particular level: it is both large and small. As Simplicius explains, both the original mixture and the homogenous stuff are unlimited: they form a whole that has everything in it, an "unlimitedly unlimited substance" (A45). All things are neither less nor more, but always equal – as a whole. Any addition to or subtraction from the sum total of the universal whole is impossible (B5):

> After these have been broken up in this way we must understand that all the things that there are are neither less nor more; for it is impossible for there to be more than all things, but all things are always as many as they are.

Since at the pre-cosmic stage of the universe "all things were together," at the present stage "everything is in everything" (B6):

And since there are equal shares in quantity of the large and small, so too there would be everything in everything; for they are not separate, but everything has a portion of everything. Since there is no least it would not be possible for there to be separation, nor for anything to exist on its own, but as at the beginning so now everything is altogether. And in everything there are many things even of what is being separated off, equal in quantity in the greater and the less.

Since every portion has the same structure and nature as the original mixture, all the generated things have a portion of all the constituent ingredients of the primary mixture, no matter what the size or the quantity is, while individual things are distinguished by the preponderance of ingredients in their structure.

The atomic theory of Leucippus and Democritus, however, took the pluralistic view in a different direction from what Empedocles' and Anaxagoras' physical theories would have anticipated. The early atomists maintained that the **atoms** and the *void* are the two fundamental principles of reality (B9). Everything, for them, consisted of imperceptible and indivisible (that is, 'a-tomic') physical units: atoms, infinite in number, which move perpetually in an infinite void (B164). Like letters and the spaces between them, which make up different texts according to their arrangement, material bodies with different biological and perceptible characteristics are made from various combinations of atoms and void; and the interesting fact about this simile is that in ancient Greek the word for 'letter' is the same as one of the words for 'principle': **stoicheion**. Different bodies are composed of the same atoms, "as tragedies and comedies are composed of the same letters" (A9). Atoms differ in shape (A from B), in position (Z from N) and in order (AN from NA) – but not in quality. Empty space or void is necessary for atomic motion. The motion of the atoms causes collisions that result either in **atomic intertwining** or in **atomic scattering**.

> ### atoms
> particles that are *atoma*, 'indivisible'

> ### stoicheion
> element; letter in the alphabet

> ### atomic intertwining
> atoms forming different compounds

> ### atomic scattering
> atoms rebounding in different directions

For the early atomists, the flux of becoming and physical alterations is incessant in the world. Generation, destruction and perceptual motion are the result of the perpetual motion of atoms in the infinite void. Whereas generation is the result of a combination of atoms, destruction is their separation. Generation is an arbitrary motion from one state of atomic conglomeration to another, through void. There would be no motion without void, and the qualitative differences in the world are dependent on the motion and quantity of the atoms. Atoms that do not have the same shape can combine to form compounds. Perceptible bodies are constructed out of atoms, and atoms move in void. Thus any impression of spatial extension is due to the material expansion of atomic compounds in space (A122).

Conclusion

The Presocratics argued about the material and formal principles on which the universe is founded. The Ionians conceived of matter as a self-developing living force (later defined as an *archē*), which can produce all animated bodies and make them reproduce. Thales initially is recorded as claiming that *water* is the primary material stuff of the universe; Anaximander postulated the *apeiron,* an unlimited and indefinite material mass as the source of everything; Anaximenes returned to Thales' monistic view and proposed *air* as the primary material principle. Other Ionians furthered this discussion of the Milesians: Xenophanes attached particular importance to *earth* and *water* in natural phenomena, and Heraclitus envisioned nature as subject to the alterations of an ever living *fire,* which produces and regulates the universe according to the hidden cosmic rhythm of the *logos.* Diogenes maintained later on that the material principle of the universe combined the characteristics of *air* and *fire.* In a radical departure from Ionian materialism, however, the Pythagoreans proposed that the cosmos is founded on *numbers* and structured according to mathematical relations. Later Presocratics such as Empedocles, Anaxagoras and Democritus denied that plurality and change derive from a single material principle, but they viewed the cosmos as a unity arising from a combination of elemental matter and forces. Empedocles accounted for change with the theory of four basic material elements — *fire, air, water and earth* — mixing and separating under the opposite cosmic

(Continued)

forces of attraction and repulsion, which he called Love and Strife. Anaxagoras introduced two cosmic principles: an initial compact mixture of elemental *ingredients* and an active formative force, *nous*, which initiated a rotation in the primordial mass and controled the subsequent expansion of the universe. Leucippus and Democritus proposed an early atomic theory, in which reality was thought to consist of innumerable imperceptible units of matter called 'atoms' from their defining property of being indivisible; these move perpetually in a boundless *void*, according to the 'necessity' of natural law.

Further Reading

Curd, P. K. (2008) "Anaxagoras and the Theory of Everything," in Curd and Graham (eds.), 230–249.

Hankinson, R. J. (2008) "Reason, Cause, and Explanation in Presocratic Philosophy," in Curd and Graham (eds.), 434–457.

Huffman, C. (1988) "The Role of Number in Philolaus' Philosophy," *Phronesis* 33: 1–30.

Lloyd, G. E. R. (1964) "Hot and Cold, Dry and Wet in Early Greek Thought," *Journal of Hellenic Studies* 84: 92–106.

Stokes, M. C. (1971) *One and Many in Presocratic Philosophy*. Harvard University Press – Center for Hellenic Studies: Cambridge, MA.

4

COSMOS

Introduction

Introduction

The Homeric world-image pictured the earth as flat and round; it was lying under the dome of the sky, called Ouranos, which was described as a solid, metallic, bowl-like hemisphere fitting over the circle of the earth (Homer, *Iliad* 17.425 and 565). The cosmic river Okeanos (Oceanus) surrounded the circular surface of the earth in an endless flux (*Iliad* 17.607; Hesiod, *Theogony* 141). The gap between the earth and the ceiling of the sky was filled with cloudy *aēr* in the lower region and with fiery *aethēr* in the upper region. Extending symmetrically downwards were Hades, Erebus and Tartarus (*Iliad* 18.13).

> ### *aēr*
> air, one of the elements, damp mist

> ### *aethēr*
> bright blue sky above misty air

Introduction to Presocratics: A Thematic Approach to Early Greek Philosophy with Key Readings, First Edition. Giannis Stamatellos.
© 2012 John Wiley & Sons, Inc. Published 2012 by John Wiley & Sons, Inc.

4.1 The Structure of the Cosmos

The Milesians had different views on the structure of the cosmos. Thales followed the Homeric world-image and described the earth as flat and round, held by water and floating on it like a log: "as a piece of wood floats on a pond, so the whole earth floats on water" (A14 and A12). Anaximander, in contrast to Thales, claimed that the earth is cylindrical in shape and compared it to a drum-like section of a stone column (A5, A11). According to him, the earth is freely suspended at the center of the universe and surrounded by three mist-covered 'wheels' – the stars, the moon and the sun – while the celestial bodies appear as 'breathing holes' of fire enclosed by the 'wheels' (A22). The stars are closest to the earth, in a circle nine times its circumference; the moon's circle is 18 times larger than the earth's; and that of the sun, which is the furthest, is 27 times larger (this is a mathematical structure using 9, 18, and 27 as ratios of 3). Another world-image is offered by Anaximenes. The earth, the sun, the moon and the other celestial bodies are flat like 'leaves' (A14–A16) that ride on a cushion of air (A20). And the celestial bodies do not move under the earth, as Anaximander believed, but they revolve around the earth like a felt cap (A7).

Xenophanes endeavored to describe the nature and structure of the earth and of the universe, as well as the place of humans in the cosmic order. He challenged Anaximander's idea of a drum-shaped earth, where life can be found on both surfaces; he supposed that we live on the top of the earth, which stretches downwards indefinitely beneath our feet. The horizontal line between air and earth is the only visible border (B28): "the upper limit of earth is seen here at our feet, in contact with air; below it stretches on and on." The sun comes from the collection of little fiery particle-clouds gathered from moist exhalations during the day (A38), while the stars are rekindled from the separation of the fiery particle-clouds at night. The sun goes infinitely onwards, even though it appears to have a circular movement due to its great distance (A41a). Xenophanes also observed the geological significance of fossils and argued, from the evidence of fossils that are found inland and on high ground, that the earth was long ago covered in mud. The human race is destroyed when the earth is covered by the sea and reappears when the earth begins to dry in the form of mud (A33).

Heraclitus emphasized the unity (B89) and homogeneity (B30) of the cosmos. The universe is an ordered and everlasting world kindled and extinguished in the fixed measures of fire (B30): "This order, the same for all, no one of gods or men has made, but it always was and is and will be, ever-living fire, kindled in measures and extinguished in measures." The celestial movements are also subject to the fixed measures of a cosmic rhythm (B100). The sun travels through the heavens in the specific measures of morning light, mid-day heat and subdued twilight (B120). The **Erinyes** guard the celestial movements and the order of the cosmos (B94). If the sun should overstep its boundaries, the universe would be thrown into a nightly abyss: "if there were no sun, as far as depended on the other stars it would be night" (B99).

> ### Erinyes
>
> Homeric avenging deities, the dark powers of Justice

The Eleatics challenged the very basis of cosmology by arguing against change, generation and plurality. In his Way of Truth, Parmenides rejected all cosmological assumptions; however, in his Way of Opinion he offered an Ionian-style cosmology with some echoes of Hesiod and Anaximander. Parmenides described a world of 'light' and 'night,' with a system of 'garlands' of light. This cosmological description is probably offered as a model of argument superior to others, but still to be rejected: it belongs in the Way of Opinion. The minimal false premise consists in posing two principles rather than one; then, if they are opposed, as 'light' and 'night' are, one might falsely generate from them all perceptible becoming. However, people have "gone astray" in naming 'light' and 'night' as two separate forms (8.55–61):

> They have distinguished them as opposites in appearance, and assigned them marks distinct from one another – to one the aetherial flame of fire, gentle and very fine, identical with itself in every direction but different from the other. The other is its opposite – dark night, a heavy and composite body. I am telling you the whole plausible arrangement of them, so that no one's thinking shall outpace you.

Thus 'light' and 'night' are the minimal opposition needed – even if only to be rejected – for the generation of the universe, since all the things are composed only of them. In this language Parmenides is preparing the way for the understanding of the 'elements,' which is to be taken further by Empedocles.

Nevertheless, the details of Parmenides' cosmology are not preserved. Perhaps, following Anaximander's image of the cosmic 'wheels' that encircle the earth, Parmenides supported a complex system of cosmic 'garlands' (*stephanoi*) that move around the earth (B12, A37). The garlands encircle each other: one is formed by the 'rare,' the other by the 'dense': the narrower one has pure fire, the wider, darkest night. Whereas the garlands of fire probably correspond to the sun and the daylight, the rings of night probably correspond to the stars and the night sky. A fire-goddess, named Justice (*Dikē*) and Necessity (*Anankē*), steers all and guides all, holding the limits of the stars in the surrounding heaven of the universe (B10). The sun itself is described as an exhalation of fire vaporized from the earth, like the circle of the Milky Way (A37). The moon is a 'night-shining,' borrowed light that wanders around the earth facing the sun (B14 and 15) – an important recognition of the fact that the moon derives its light from the sun, later followed by Empedocles (B42 and B43).

Anaxagoras reaffirmed the importance of cosmology. He regarded the sky as his homeland (A1) and believed that the most important thing in life was to contemplate the heavens and the whole order of the universe (A30). Anaxagoras maintained, like Thales, that the earth is flat in shape and, like Anaximander, that it remains suspended at the center of the universe. Its size enables it to ride on air, as Anaximenes had proposed, and there would be no empty space through which it could fall, just as the Eleatics claimed (A42, A88). Anaxagoras introduced the radical view that the sun, the moon and the stars are hot stones held together by the strong circular motion of the *aethēr* (A1, A12 and A42). In his cosmology the sun is a hot stone larger than the Peloponnese, and the moon has dwelling places, hills and ravines (A1).

Anaxagoras followed Parmenides and Empedocles in claiming that the moon receives its light from the sun (B18) and that the stars shine as a result of the resistance and whirling of the *aethēr* (A12, A19). However, the heat of the stars is not perceptible, and this is due to their distance from the earth and to the fact that they occupy cooler places in the cosmos (A42). The moon is closer to the earth than the sun and the stars around the earth; below the stars there are other invisible celestial bodies, which rotate along with the visible ones (A42). The Milky Way is the reflection of the light of those stars, which are not illuminated by the sun (A42). The comets are conglomerations of planets that throw out flames (A1).

Anaxagoras also attempted explanations of the natural phenomena and of the origins of species. An earthquake is the sinking of air into the earth (A1, A89) and the winds are caused by the rarefaction of the air produced by the sun (A1, A42). He explained thunder and lightning through the physical activity of clouds: while thunder is a clashing of clouds, lightning results from their friction (A1, A42 and A84). He supported the view that animals were generated from a mixture of moist, hot and earthly stuffs (A1, A42), and he explained the saltiness and bitterness of the sea as consequences of its evaporation under the sun (A90). He also had the idea that humans inhabit places on earth unknown to us, where they live and produce like us (B4). Time, for Anaxagoras, is an essential factor in the development of things; an extensive period of time, for example, could result in tremendous changes in the surrounding environment, such as the mountains becoming seas (A1).

4.2   The Formation of the Cosmos

Anaximander claimed that all things in the universe originate from the everlasting source of the *apeiron* (A10). His cosmogony is a step towards discriminating between an eternal and a temporal condition of the universe: the *apeiron* is the origin of temporal becoming, which preserves in its turn the everlastingness of its source in different recurring temporal conditions. Anaximander's *apeiron* could be an elaboration of Hesiod's primeval *chaos*. In the first separation of the opposites from the *apeiron*, something capable of producing heat and cold emerged (A10); and Anaximander's heat and cold resemble Hesiod's Eros and Earth respectively. The earth, which is cold and heavy, stays still in equilibrium at the centre of the universe (A26).

Whereas Heraclitus described the formation of universe as the work of an ever-living fire 'kindled' and 'extinguished' in fixed measures (B30), Empedocles described this creative process as an eternal production that happens in two successive but opposing phases: one corresponding to the increasing dominance of Love and to the mixing of the four elements, the other to the increasing dominance of Strife and to the separation the elements (B26):

> They prevail in turn as the cycle moves round, and decrease into each other and increase in appointed succession. For these are the only real things, and, as they run through one another, they become men and the kinds of other animals – at one time coming into one order through love, at another again being borne away from each other by strife's hate, until they come together into the whole and are subdued. So, insofar as one is

accustomed to arise from many, and many are produced from one as it is again being divided, to this extent they are born and have no abiding life; but insofar as they never cease their continual exchange, they are for ever unaltered in the cycle.

However, Empedocles maintained that generation could not be creation from nothing, nor destruction complete separation into nothing: generation was to be explained as the *mixing* of the four elements by the act of Love, while destruction, as the *separation* of the four elements under the act of Strife (B12).

Anaxagoras claimed that in the beginning of the cosmos everything was combined, in a complete and uniform fusion of all the elementary stuffs: the seeds (*spermata*) of all things were infinite and nothing could be distinguished from anything except the prevailing air and *aethēr* (B1):

> All things were together, unlimited in number and smallness; and even the small was unlimited, and, all things being together, nothing was distinct because of its smallness. For air and *aethēr* covered everything, both being unlimited. For these are the greatest in all things, both in quantity and size.

The formation of the cosmos started when the elementary stuffs were separated from the original mixture, in a vortex initiated by the motive power of *nous* (B12):

> Mind knew all that had been mixed and was being separated and becoming distinct. And all that was going to be, all that was but is no longer, and all that is now and will be, mind arranged in order, and this rotation too, in which now rotate the stars and sun and moon and air and *aethēr*, as they are being separated off. And it was the rotation that caused the separation. The dense is being separated off from the rare, and the hot from the cold, the bright from the dark and the dry from the wet.

Air and *aethēr* were the first to be separated out, as perceptible elements, from the quantity of the surrounding mass, which was also infinite in amount (B2). The cosmic rotation of the material ingredients resulted in the predominantly heavy parts moving towards to the centre of the vortex and the fine parts to the outer part (B15): "The thick and the wet and the cold and the dark came together, and there is now earth; the fine and the hot and the dry moved out towards the furthest part of the *aethēr*." Under the control of *nous* the universe expands continually and indefinitely outwards from the original microdot, which contained in miniature everything there is in the cosmos. The totality of the cosmos remains in an integrated and uniform completeness (B8): "the contents of the one cosmos are not separated from each other or cut of by an axe – not the hot from the cold nor the cold from the hot." Thus the cosmos is explained, for Anaxagoras, not in terms of the transformation of a limited number of finite elements, as it is for Empedocles, but by the expanding rearrangement of a predominant portion of infinite and eternally existing elementary ingredients.

Leucippus and Democritus envisaged, like Anaxagoras, a universe containing a plurality of worlds – an open universe with numerous solar systems and galaxies, extending in infinite space through an eternal cycle of generation and destruction, whereby different world-systems repeatedly arise and disintegrate. Whereas Anaxagoras introduced an expanding universe that began from an original mixture, the atomists inaugurated an ever-existing universe of infinite extent. Given infinite atomic material and limitless void, numerous worlds are continually being formed, maturing and disintegrating.

On the basis of Diogenes Laertius' testimony (9.31), the atomic cosmogony could be briefly described as follows. Atoms move randomly in the void. Some atoms with compatible movements come together and start a vortex. As a result of the collision of similar atom groups through the vortex, atoms are caught up in various rotations and then begin to separate off. Atoms rotate in equilibrium, abiding together and getting intertwined; thus they make up an initial sphere. The sphere moves apart, surrounded by a cosmic membrane that encloses all sorts of bodies within it. Due to counter-pressure from the centre of the membrane, bodies whirl around. Due to the rotation of bodies, the surrounding membrane whirls. The bodies adjacent to the membrane are continually drawn into the vortex. The earth is created when the bodies come together to the centre of the membrane. The membrane expands with the intrusion of the outside bodies as it moves around the vortex. The outside bodies become intertwined with the membrane and produce some original moist and muddy cosmic structures, which dry out later at the outer surface of the vortex, ending up as the substance of the stars.

4.3 Cosmos and Harmony

Pythagoras is said to have been the first to use the term **kosmos** for the 'sum of the whole' as

> **kosmos**
>
> order, arrangement; the derivative noun *kosmēma* means 'jewel'

an ordered, beautiful and harmonious world (Aetius 2.1.1). The whole universe is modeled on numbers, and the heaven is arranged in the harmonious correlation of mathematical relations. The Pythagoreans maintained that all the properties of numbers are expressed in the attributes and parts of the universal harmony in the form of unity and order (Aristotle, *Metaphysics* 985^{b}31–6^{a}6). Music is the finest expression of the mathematical cosmos in the musical harmony of the heavenly spheres. According to Aristotle (*De caelo* 290^{b}12), the Pythagorean theory of the harmony of the spheres is based on the fact that the motion of every physical body produces a kind of sound. The Pythagoreans therefore maintained that the celestial bodies would produce sounds resulting from the speed of their concentric movement around of the centre of the cosmos. The motion of the celestial bodies is measured by the same ratios as those that express the musical intervals of concordances or harmonies, and these ratios are derived from limit and unlimited (Philolaus B1).

The Pythagorean universe is unique (Stobaeus 1.18.1): "from the infinite it draws in time, breath and void, which distinguishes the places of separate things." The heavens are generated in a limited temporality, which in turn derives from an eternal and 'unlimited breath': the *pneuma* that surrounds the universe (B30). The cosmos is an eternal living organism that breathes in and out, inhaling (*anapnein*) and exhaling the surrounding void (*kenon*) (Aristotle, *Physics* 213^b). The cosmic void extends infinitely in every direction throughout the spherical cosmos, and the structure of universal order originates in the dynamic application of the finite numbers to the infinitude of *pneuma* (B26).

The Pythagoreans offered significant cosmological observations. They claimed that the shape of the earth is spherical, they added the five celestial zones and they identified the evening star with the morning star (Diogenes Laertius 8.48 and 9.23, Aetius 3.14.1). It is also noteworthy that the early Pythagoreans denied the geocentric and geostatic model of the universe. According to the testimony of Aristotle (*De caelo* 293^{a}18), they placed *fire* and not earth at the centre of the universe. The earth became a celestial body, which creates day and night by its circular motion around **Hestia** (*hestia* meaning 'heath'). Ten divine celestial bodies – ten being the perfect number, which encompasses the whole nature of numbers – rotate rhythmically around Hestia in the following order: the dark counter-earth (*antichthōn*),

> **Hestia**
>
> central cosmic fire, the hearth of the world

the earth, the moon, the sun, the five planets (Saturn, Jupiter, Mars, Venus, Mercury) and the sphere of the fixed stars (Aristotle, *Metaphysics* 986ᵃ). This new cosmological model is usually attributed to Philolaus (B7 and A16) and explained through the importance of the Monad in Pythagorean metaphysics. Since the Monad is the divine source of all numbers and is identified with, or represented by, the purity of fire, the source of the celestial bodies should be a divine fire in the centre of the cosmos (Aristotle, *Metaphysics* 986ᵃ).

Conclusion

A plurality of views can be found in Presocratic cosmologies, which are based initially on geocentric models. For Thales, the earth is flat and round, supported by the water on which it floats. Anaximander described the earth as cylindrical, drum-like in shape, freely suspended at the centre of the world and surrounded by the sun, the moon and the stars, which were conceived of as points of light in mist-covered 'wheels.' Anaximenes described the earth and the other celestial bodies as flat, leaf-like shapes that ride on air. In response to Anaximander's image of a drum-shaped earth that hosts life on both its surfaces, Xenophanes supposed that the earth stretches downwards indefinitely beneath our feet. Heraclitus stressed the unity, homogeneity and everlastingness of the cosmos. The world order is maintained by an ever-lasting fire, kindled and extinguished in fixed measures. In his Way of Truth, Parmenides argued against all cosmological assumptions, but in the part of his poem known as the Way of Opinion he constructed a world of 'light' and 'night,' with the help of a complex system of 'garlands' of light comparable to the 'wheels' in Anaximander's cosmology. Empedocles envisioned the cosmos as being caught in recurring cycles of eternal generation and destruction, under forces of attraction and repulsion, whereas Anaxagoras proposed one single cosmos, ever expanding from an initial vortex generated by *nous* in the primordial mixture. The Pythagoreans were the first to remove the earth from its central position in the universe, and they replaced

(Continued)

it with the 'hearth of fire.' The earth, along with the other visible celestial bodies and a dark 'counter-earth,' was then thought to rotate around the fire of Hestia, and this circular motion took place according to a rhythmic order of mathematical perfection. In contrast to all these previous cosmologies, the open universe of Leucippus and Democritus, with its infinite supply of atoms in a limitless space, gave rise to the constant and simultaneous generation and dissolution of a plurality of solar systems and galaxies extending through the void.

Further Reading

Algra, K. (1999) "The Beginnings of Cosmology," in Long, 45–65.

Furley, D. J. (1987) *The Greek Cosmologists*, Vol. 1: *The Formation of the Atomic Theory and its Earliest Critics*. Cambridge: Cambridge University Press.

Kahn, C. H. (1960) *Anaximander and the Origins of Greek Cosmology*. Columbia University Press.

Raven, J. E. (1954) "The Basis of Anaxagoras' Cosmology," *Classical Quarterly* 4: 123–137.

Trépanier, S. (2003) "Empedocles on the Ultimate Symmetry of the World," *Oxford Studies in Ancient Philosophy* 24: 1–58.

Wright, M. R. (2008) "Presocratic Cosmologies," in Curd and Graham, 413–433.

5
BEING

Introduction
5.1 Being and Not-Being
5.2 The Unity of Being
5.3 Paradoxes of Motion
5.4 Being and Infinity
Conclusion

Introduction

Plato recognized Parmenides as the thinker who differentiated his philosophy from that of the Ionians (*Sophist* 180e, 237a). Whereas the Ionians were interested in the generation and structure of the material world and in the nature of becoming, Parmenides and the Eleatics focused on the nature of **being**. Parmenides denied plurality and change in the phenomenal world; he claimed instead that there is only one, unified, timeless and undifferentiated being. Parmenides had an influence on Zeno's paradoxes of motion and on Melissus' notion of being. The Eleatic ideas about being are also reflected in Empedocles' physical theory and in the early version of atomism developed by Leucippus and Democritus.

> **being**
>
> *to* (*e*)*on*, what is

Introduction to Presocratics: A Thematic Approach to Early Greek Philosophy with Key Readings, First Edition. Giannis Stamatellos.
© 2012 John Wiley & Sons, Inc. Published 2012 by John Wiley & Sons, Inc.

5.1   Being and Not-Being

The signs (**sēmata**) of being, or its predicates, are stated in the eighth extant fragment of Parmenides' poem *On Nature*: being is ungenerated,

> **sēmata**
>
> signs; in this case, the signs of being

indestructible, unique, unmoved, unchanging, timeless, continuous, and complete in itself. Being is un-extended in time and un-expanded in space; it is universally equal to itself and uniformly determined. In the prologue of his poem, Parmenides argued (in the words of the goddess of truth) that the true nature of being is to be found by following a certain way of reasoning (B2):

> Come now, pay heed to my account and take it with you – I shall tell you only the ways of enquiry that are to be thought of: that it is and cannot not be is the path of persuasion, for it attends on truth, that it is not, and necessarily is not, is, I tell you, a path of which nothing can be learnt, for you could not recognise what is not (that is impossible) nor name it [...]

Thus the appropriate "way of enquiry" is [P1] to accept that "it is and cannot not be" (and this is the path of being); and [P2] to reject that "it is not, and necessarily is not" (the path of not-being). A compromise [P3] between the two paths – "to be and not to be the same and not the same" (B6.8) – is also to be rejected: only one path leads us to true being. Parmenides' argument may be briefly analyzed as follows.

The path of *not-being* [P2] is a non-starter. Since what-is-not *is not*, not-being is inconceivable and unknowable (B8.17). If we are going to think and speak rationally, there must be an object of thought and speech that necessarily exists, given that only being *is* and not-being *is not* (B6.1–2).

The compromise way, in which *being and not-being* are valid simultaneously [P3], is also rejected. Two contradictory ontological conditions cannot be true for the same subject at the same time (B6.3–9). However, for Parmenides, despite the logical absurdity some thinkers accept the contradictory ontological simultaneity of being and not-being. This criticism seems to be particularly directed at some Ionian or Heraclitean philosophers (or even at Heraclitus himself), who "move along deaf as well as blind, dazed uncritical crowds, who consider to be and not to be the same and not the same, and that for all things there is a path turning back again" (B6.7–9). Whereas for Heraclitus one opposite condition (A) *presupposes* the other (not-A) – in other words, contradiction justifies the unity of being – for Parmenides one opposite condition (A) *excludes* the other (not-A) – in other words, contradiction justifies the denial of not-being. So, for Parmenides, any plurality, even the minimal one represented by two, is impossible.

Parmenides concludes that the true path points to an *unqualified being* [P1], which is one, unified, all alike, indivisible and continuous (B8):

> It is not divisible, since it is all alike; nor is there more [of it] at one time and less at another, which would prevent its continuity, but all is full of what there is. So that it all holds together, for what-is stays close to what-is. (22–5)

True being is without beginning or end, generation or destruction; for these involve a preceding or a subsequent state of *is-not* and, a fortiori, the succession of starts and stops involved in change cannot reside in true being (B8):

> Moreover, without beginning and without end (since generation and destruction have been driven afar, and true conviction has cast them out), it is immobile in the bonds of great chains. Remaining the same and in the same, it abides by itself and so stays firm, for harsh necessity keeps it in the chains of the limit which holds it around, because it is not right for what-is to be incomplete; for it is not in need – if it were it would need everything. (26–35)

Since not-being is rejected, true being should be conceived of as undivided, without any internal differentiation or contradiction, timeless, indestructible, unchangeable, immobile, complete and equal to itself, outside any spatial application.

Summarizing Parmenides' argument: speech and thought require their subject 'to be.' Since 'not-being' should be rejected as absurd [P2] and the putting together of 'being' and 'not-being' is contradictory [P3], the only true option that remains is 'being' [P1]. True being or *what-is* should have 'no beginning' (that would need the not-being before being, which is rejected) and 'no end' (that would need the not-being after it, which is equally rejected). Nor could what-is change (e.g. red to not-red to not-green to green), as change brings in a series of temporal not-being. Additionally, what-is cannot move, as this requires spatial not-being, which is again unacceptable. Therefore true being, or what-really-is, is one, timeless, complete and unchanging.

Parmenides' radical conception of being later influenced Empedocles' physical theory. Nevertheless, Empedocles moved a step forward. He reconciled Parmenides' monism of being with the Ionian hylozoism of becoming in an ontological synthesis. On the one hand, Empedocles followed Parmenides' theory of being with regard to the generation and destruction for what really exists, but, on the other hand, he accepted the Ionian concept of becoming as an internal and continual reor-ganization of the material constituents of being. Whereas being remains ontologically indestructi-ble, becoming is manifest in the plurality of mortal beings. Furthermore, Empedocles accepted Parmenides' denial of not-being as empty space, which he calls **kenon** – the term by which the early Atomists will des-ignate the void.

> **kenon**
>
> void, empty space, vacuum

For Leucippus and Democritus, the atoms are the new 'being,' while void proves that not-being is as real as 'being' (A6):

> Leucippus and his associate Democritus spoke of 'the full' and 'the empty' as elements, calling the one – the full and solid –'what is,' and the other – the empty – 'what is not,' and that is why they say that what is is no more than what is not, and that 'empty' is as real as body.

Since there is no part of the whole that is empty or overfull, the whole is a *plenum*: "it is impossible for there to be coming into existence from what is not, and for what exists to be completely destroyed cannot be achieved, and is unheard of; for where it is thrust at any time, there it will always" (B12). Not-being exists as emptiness: 'what-is' is the *plenum* of atoms, while 'what-is-not' (*to mēden*) is the *vacuum* of void (*to kenon*). Whereas the atoms are infinite in number, void is infinite in extent. However, both atoms and void are equally existent. On the one hand, atoms are infinite in number, indivisible, indestructible and solid units or particles of matter, imperceptible due to their smallness. On the other hand, void signifies the infinite emptiness of the universe in which atoms move and arrange. Thus the early theory of atoms should be regarded as a direct reply to the Eleatic denial of not-being, and particularly to Zeno's arguments against the plurality of things and against the infinite divisibility of spatial extension, which are briefly presented in the next sections.

5.2 The Unity of Being

In order to support the unity of being, Zeno, Parmenides' pupil, brings the following questions to bear against the plurality of things. If there are many things and not just one:

[Q1] How many are they?
[Q2] What size do they have?
[Q3] Can we perceive them with our senses?
[Q4] Where are they? Do they move?

Zeno's aim is to show the absurd and untenable conclusions that result from a possible denial of Parmenides' position – his claim for one and unchanging being. Zeno refutes the seemingly obvious assumptions about the plurality and mobility of things through the following replies.

Reply to Q1 Zeno argues against the plurality of things through the antinomy of the following hypothetical syllogisms (B3). [1.1] If there are many things, then they will be just as many as they are, no more and no less. Therefore existing things are limited in number. [1.2] If there are many things, there will always be other things between them to distinguish them, and again others between them *ad infinitum*. Therefore existing things are unlimited in number. Thus [1.1] and [1.2] lead us to the contradictory conclusion that, if there are many things, they are both limited and unlimited in number.

Reply to Q2 Zeno argues similarly against spatial extension in the following dilemma (B1 and B2). [2.1] If something has no size, it would be nothing. If something with no size is added to, or subtracted from, something with size, it would not make it any bigger or smaller. [2.2] If there are many things, then either they are so small as to have no size, and so they are nothing, or they have some size, which makes them infinitely big. Thus [2.1] and [2.2] lead us again to the contradictory conclusion that, if there are many beings, they must be both small and great – so small as to have no size and so big as to be unlimited in size.

Reply to Q3 Zeno (A29) replies with the example of the 'millet seed,' in a short dialogue with Protagoras reported by Simplicius:

ZENO: Tell me Protagoras, does a single millet seed make a noise as it falls, or does 1/10,000 of a millet?
PROTAGORAS: No.

ZENO:	Does a bushel of millet seed make a noise as it falls, or not?
PROTAGORAS:	Yes, a bushel makes a noise.
ZENO:	But isn't there a ratio (*logos*) between a bushel of millet seed and one seed, or 1/10,000 of a seed?
PROTAGORAS:	Yes, there is.
ZENO:	So won't there be the same ratio of sounds between them, for the sounds are in proportion to what makes the sound? And, if this is so, if the bushel of millet seed makes a noise, so will a single seed and 1/10,000 of a seed.

The conclusion is that, because of the weakness of our perception, it is impossible for us to mark a division in the series running from one seed to a bushel when a sound is heard, although it is heard.

Reply to Q4   Zeno argues against spatial extension through the following argument (B4). What moves is moving either in the place where it is, so it is at rest, or in the place in which it is not, which is not possible. This leads us to the absurd conclusion that what moves is at rest, hence what moves is *not* moving.

5.3   Paradoxes of Motion

Zeno's four paradoxes of motion, which survive in Aristotle's brief exposition in *Physics* 239^b9–40^a1 (A25–A28), deal with difficulties in supposing that movement exists. Zeno's aim is to support Parmenides' thesis that being must be one and immovable.

THE DICHOTOMY PARADOX: it is impossible
to move from one place to another

The first argument about there being no movement says that the moving object must first reach the halfway mark before the end – and the quarter-mark before the half, and so back, so there is no first move; and the three-quarter mark after the half, and so forward, so that there is no last move. (A25)

In the first paradox Zeno illustrates the problem of the infinite divisibility of spatial extension. For him, motion in a finite time is impossible on account of the infinite divisibility of space. His example is that of an athlete who is unable to run the set length of a stadium track. Suppose the athlete has to run from the starting point A to the end point B. The athlete has to travel first to the halfway point C, and then go from there to B. But, if D is the halfway point between C and B, the athlete must run to D first; and so on, *ad infinitum*. Zeno concludes that it is impossible for the athlete to accomplish an infinite number of halfway points in finite time. Therefore the athlete cannot complete a movement over a set distance and reach the finishing line.

THE PARADOX OF ACHILLES AND THE TORTOISE:
Achilles cannot overtake the tortoise

The second is the one called Achilles. This is it: the slowest will never be overtaken in running by the fastest, for the pursuer must always come to the point the pursued has left, so that the slower must always be some (proportionate) distance ahead. (A26)

In the second paradox, Zeno presents a more complex version of the first, introducing two moving objects. Here the purpose of the runner is neither to cover a set distance nor to reach a finishing line, but to overtake another, who is on the move as well. When Achilles (the faster runner) has reached the tortoise at point P1, the tortoise will be at the next point, P2; when Achilles reaches P2, the tortoise will be at P3 – and so on, *ad infinitum*. Zeno concludes that, despite the fact that the distances between Achilles and the tortoise will continually decrease, the tortoise will always be one move ahead. Therefore "the slowest will never be overtaken in running by the fastest, for the pursuer must always come to the point which the pursued has left, so that the slower must always be some distance ahead" (A26).

THE ARROW PARADOX: the moving arrow is at rest

The third [paradox] [...] is that the moving arrow is at rest. The arrow is at rest at any time when it occupies a space just its own length, and yet it is always moving at any time in its flight (i.e. in the 'now'), therefore the moving arrow is motionless. (A27)

This paradox illustrates the impossibility of motion in time. Suppose that time consists of a series of moments ('nows,' *to nun*). The arrow is moving at any moment or 'now' during its flight. At any moment – in the 'now' – the arrow is at rest, that is, it occupies no more than its own length. But if the moving arrow is at rest at any moment during its flight, this contradicts our perception that the arrow is moving at every moment of its flight.

THE STADIUM PARADOX: a period of time is twice its own duration

The fourth [paradox] is the one about equal blocks moving past equal blocks from opposite directions in the stadium – one set from the end of the stadium and one from the middle – at the same speed; here he thinks that half the time is equal to twice itself. For example: AAAA are equal stationary blocks, BBBB, equal to them in number and size, are beginning from the half-way point (of the stadium), CCCC equal to these also in size, and equal to the Bs in speed, are coming towards them from the end. It happens of course that the first B reaches the end at the same time as the first C as they move past each other. And it happens that the C passes all the Bs but the Bs only half (the As) so the time is then half itself. (A28)

The fourth paradox highlights the problem of motion in time. Suppose that in a stadium there are three equal sets of contiguous blocks A, B and C. Set A is stationary. Sets B and C move at equal speeds, past each other and past set A, in opposite directions. While one block of set B takes time t to traverse past two blocks of set C, it takes $2t$ to traverse two block of set A. This leads to the absurd conclusion that time t is equal to time $2t$, which is the double amount of time.

On the basis of the above paradoxes, Zeno argues that plurality and mobility lead to a series of absurdities involving the infinite divisibility of spatial extension, the impossibility of motion in time and the unreliability of sense perception. These questions were taken up again by Melissus of Samos.

5.4   Being and Infinity

Melissus supported Parmenides' theory of being, agreeing that generation and destruction, birth and death, beginning and end in time presuppose prior and posterior states of not-being, and so must be denied true
being. However, Melissus' important contribution is the notion of the
infinity of being as regards its temporal everlastingness and spatial limitlessness: being is "eternal and without limit, and one and a homogenous whole" (B7). Whereas Parmenides had argued for a finite,
sphere-like being, which is unchanging, complete, continuous, equal to
itself on every side and resting uniformly in its limits (B8.42–49),
Melissus accepts an unchanging, complete, immobile, being, with no
gaps or variation in density, but he gives it no defined limit or boundary.
Since limit presupposes two points to be defined (a limiting and a
limited), whereas being has to be one and homogenous (B7), being has
to be without limits (B6): "For if it were without limit, it would be one;
for, if there were two, they could not be without limit, but one would
limit the other."

Parmenides' being never *was*, in the past, never *will be*, in the future,
but *is* – now, in a timeless present – while Melissus' being *is*, always *was*
and always *will be*, in eternity (B1): "What was always was and always
shall be, for, if it came into being, before its generation there would have
to be nothing; therefore, if there were nothing, nothing at all would come
from nothing." For Melissus, the denial of not-being leads to the conclusion that being is eternal not in terms of an atemporal timelessness (as
in Parmenides), but in terms of an enduring but tensed existence. Since
being is ungenerated, it has no temporal beginning; and, since it is indestructible, it has no temporal end. Since being neither began nor ended,
it always was and always will be, everlastingly (B2):

> Since then it did not come into being, it is and always was and always
> shall be, and has neither beginning nor end, but is without limit. For if it
> had come into being, it would have a beginning (for it would have begun
> to come into being at some time) and an end (for it would have stopped
> coming into being at some time); but, since it neither began nor ended, it
> always was and shall be and has no beginning nor end; for it is impossible
> for the incomplete to be everlasting.

While Parmenides' being is tenseless, in the 'now,' Melissus' being is
eternal (B4): "no thing that has both beginning and end is eternal or
without limit."

Moreover, Melissus denies spatial division and limit. Since not-being is refuted, what-is must be conceived of as unlimited not only temporally, but also as spatially: "but as it always is, so it is also without limit in extent" (B3). Since being is unchanging, full and homogenous, there is no space in which one could differentiate a distinct corporeal unity within unlimited extension. Since thickness and bulk presuppose division into parts, what-is will no longer be single, but plural (B9): "So if it exists it must be one; and being one it could not have body. If it had thickness it would have parts and would no longer be one." Any division into parts entails change, which is contradicted by the truth of existence and being (B10): "if what exists is divided, it moves: and if it moves it would not exist." On the basis of the above considerations, Melissus adopts the radical position that whatever exists is limitlessly extended in space, since empty units breaking the homogeneity of being are impossible (B7). From this position it is deduced that being must be conceived of as intangible and shapeless in physical corporeality, and complete in space and time.

Finally, Melissus deduces a series of refutations concerning change, alteration and perceptible phenomena. These refutations survive in a long text preserved in Simplicius (B7). Since being is eternal, unlimited and homogenous, it follows that *what really is* must be identified as being (1) without change in time; (2) without internal rearrangement in order and structure; (3) without pain or distress; and (4) without emptiness and movement.

Conclusion

Being was the main topic of inquiry for the Eleatic philosophers. In opposition to the Ionian flux of temporal becoming, Parmenides supported the stability and timelessness of being (*what–is*). However, Parmenides' philosophy of being aimed also to explain the genuine nature of things, which fits with the explorations of nature found in other Presocratics. Parmenides denied not-being as self-contradictory and accepted, as the conclusion of a deductive process, the existence of an unqualified and uniformly determined being, which is ungenerated, indestructible, unique, unmoved, unchanging, continuous and complete. There is no birth and death, spatial extension, or past and future, but what there is is "now, all at once." Parmenides' pupil, Zeno of Elea, defended his master's thesis in a series of paradoxes of motion and refutations of plurality. Melissus of Samos developed Parmenides' notion of being by introducing the infinity of being in terms of temporal everlastingness and spatial limitlessness. Empedocles reconciled Ionian becoming with Eleatic being in an ontological synthesis. Whereas the being of the world as a whole remains indestructible through its cycles, birth and death are to be viewed as mixtures and separations of four immortal and unchanging elements, under the formative force of Love and the destructive force of Strife. Finally, Leucippus and Democritus claimed atoms as the new 'being,' but they also asserted that void, conceived of as empty space and 'not-being,' proves that not-being is as real and existing as 'being.'

Further Reading

Barnes, J. (1979) "Parmenides and the Eleatic One," *Archiv für Geschichte der Philosophie* 61: 1–21.

Furth, M. (1974) "Elements of Eleatic Ontology," in Mourelatos (ed.), 241–270.

Furley, D. J. (1974) "Zeno and Invisible Magnitudes," in Mourelatos (ed.), 353–367.

McKirahan, R. D. (1999) "Zeno," in Long (ed.), 134–158.

McKirahan, R. D. (2008) "Signs and Arguments in Parmenides B8," in Curd and Graham (eds.), 189–229.

Owen, G. E. L. (1960) "Eleatic Questions," *Classical Quarterly* 10: 84–102.

Sedley, D. (1999) "Parmenides and Melissus," in Long (ed.), 113–133.

SOUL

Introduction

In the Homeric poems the living body, the man himself, is destroyed at death, while the soul (*psuchē*) survives, leading a shadowy existence in Hades. The Homeric *psuchē* descends to the underworld, in the manner of dreams taking wing (*Odyssey* 11.224) and of ghostly twittering bats (*Odyssey* 24.6–9). In Hades the *psuchē* has recognizable features, but no meaningful speech (*Odyssey* 11). Life after death is a state of decline compared with life on earth, in the world of mortals (*Odyssey* 11.465–540). Even glorified heroes, like Achilles, wonder with nostalgia about their earthly life: "I'd rather serve as another man's laborer, as a poor peasant without land, and be alive on Earth, than be lord of all the lifeless dead" (*Odyssey* 11.465–540). However, the Presocratic *psuchē* shifted its meaning, from designating the Homeric flitting shade in Hades to representing the source of life and intelligence, both at the human and at the cosmic level. The problem of body and soul in relation to life, death and transmigration is discussed, particularly by the Pythagoreans, and a new perception of time and idea of immortality is introduced by some Presocratic thinkers.

Introduction to Presocratics: A Thematic Approach to Early Greek Philosophy with Key Readings, First Edition. Giannis Stamatellos.
© 2012 John Wiley & Sons, Inc. Published 2012 by John Wiley & Sons, Inc.

6.1 Life and Intelligence

The Ionian thinkers connected the soul with the primal substance of the universe. Thales probably maintained that the substance of the soul is water (A1). Since, for Thales, water is the divine vital source of all living things, and since all things are alive, the vital power of the soul is intermingled in the universe, and Thales could claim that the whole world is "full of gods" (A22). From the example of the magnet, Thales inferred that even seemingly non-living things, such as stones, are alive (A1 and A22). Anaximenes similarly connected *psuchē* to the principle of air and the breath of life that binds and maintains both human life and the cosmos: "as our soul, which is air, maintains us, so breath and air surround the whole world" (B2).

Heraclitus connected the soul to fire: *psuchē* is a fiery substance subject to physical alterations (B36): "For souls it is death to become water, for water death to become earth; from earth arises water, and from water soul." The soul dies in water and arises from it following the 'changes' of fire (B31): "The changes of fire: first sea, and of sea half earth and half lightning flash; earth is poured out as sea and is measured in the same proportion as it was before it became earth." Whereas for Thales water is related to life and *psuchē*, for Heraclitus water is the *opposite* to living fire (B77). The entrance of water into the fiery soul decreases its power and means the beginning of the soul's death. Fire is the physical aspect of *logos* and, in the Heraclitean world of opposition, the soul experiences the conflict and resolution of the different tensions of contradictory feelings: it is through illness that we realize the importance of health, after hunger satiety is welcome, and weariness makes us appreciate the end of work (B111). The soul is at rest in the constant change of harmonious opposition (B84a).

Empedocles described the soul as being composed of the four elements, and he called it a spirit (*daimōn*) of divine origin. He related physical structure to psychical structure and maintained that the latter is determined by the former, since intelligence is dependent on the mixture of elements in the heart blood (B105): "<the heart is> nourished in seas of blood coursing to and fro, and there above all is what humans call thought, because, for humans, blood around the heart does the thinking." An internal change of structure results in a change of thought (B108), and external conditions affect the internal structure (B106). Hence, for Empedocles, wisdom results from the corresponding balance of structure between the elements (the physical) and thought (the psychical), which is attained through intellectual effort and physical practice.

While for Empedocles (in B105) – and for ancient Greeks generally – the heart area was central to life and intelligence, since injury to the heart brings death and emotions like fear and anger affect it, the Pythagorean Alcmaeon is the first recorded thinker to propose the *brain* as the seat of consciousness and intelligence (A5). Alcmaeon maintained that the brain includes the channels through which sense-perception operates. Another Pythagorean, Philolaus of Croton, placed the soul in the heart but, following Alcmaeon, he too regarded the head as the seat of intellect (B13).

Anaxagoras focused on human mind as an independent principle, responsible for the control both of our physical body and of our cognitive faculties. For Anaxagoras, the human mind is related to *psuchē* and intelligence, and it has the same structure and substance as the cosmic *nous* – the active vital force, the purest and most rarefied of all things (B12): "all that has *psuchē*, whether larger or smaller, mind controls; and mind controlled the rotation of the whole, so as to make it rotate in the beginning." Anaxagoras' conception of *nous* oscillates between material and immaterial. Whereas *nous* has a physical basis, Anaxagoras stretches language in trying to express its immaterial aspects. *Nous* is independent, that is, not *physically* mixed with anything else, since any possible physical mixture will diminish its purity, knowledge, infinite power and control. However, in everything there is a portion of everything *except of mind*; but some beings have mind as well (B11).

Anaxagoras' conception of the mental activity of *nous* has a physical aspect, which could be also found earlier in Parmenides and in the physical correlation given between the thinking subject and its objects, both made of fire and night. Fire and night constitute the composition of different thoughts (B16): "according to the nature of the mixture of the wandering limbs that each one has, so does thought stand for each; that which thinks, the nature of the limbs, is the same for each and everyone; and what there is more of is that thought."

However, it has to be noted that Anaxagoras' theory of *nous* received some criticism in the classical age. In Plato's *Phaedo* 97b–99c, Socrates, despite his initial enthusiasm for Anaxagoras' book, appears to be disappointed to find that Anaxagoras' *nous* was not presented as actually responsible for the final ordering of things for the best, but only for the structure of material elements such as air, *aethēr* and water (A47). Likewise, at *Metaphysics* 985ᵃ18, Aristotle criticized Anaxagoras for using *nous* as a cosmogonical **deus ex machina**: according to him, *nous* was introduced as a device to disguise Anaxagoras' inability to explain the real causes of things (A47).

> **deus ex machina**
>
> god from the machine, i.e. from a theatrical device that allowed divine characters to appear on stage as if by miracle; a supreme agent (or God) provides an unexpected solution to an unsolved problem

The early atomists had a strictly materialistic conception of the *psuchē*. Like everything else, the soul is made of atoms moving in void, but of atoms that move swiftly because of their small size and spherical shape (A101). Spherical atoms compose the fire and the soul; in the air, too, there is a great number of atoms of that kind, and, as Aristotle reports, "that is why life and death depend on breathing in and out" (A106). At death the atoms disperse and may re-group into other compounds (A106). Democritus claimed that an individual person is a miniature cosmos (B34) and that the soul is the source of bodily motion (A108) and intelligence (A107). Human intelligence depends on the alterations and movements of primary particles within individual bodies, and also on contact with other particles, external to them.

Diogenes of Apollonia related *aēr* (air) both to life (following Anaximenes) and to intelligence. Life and intelligence are the two inter-related functions of the *psuchē*: breath and thought, conceived of as correlated organic–cognitive activities of the soul (B3 and B4). Air controls all things as an intelligent principle that animates the cosmos and provides consciousness and reason to the soul (B5). Whereas mortal beings are subject to becoming, air is an eternal and immortal body, endowed with knowledge and perception (B7 and B8). Diogenes further offers an analogy between body and mind, physiology and cognition, which establishes the ontological and biological origins and structure of the individual body and of the cosmos (A19).

6.2 Transmigration

Whereas for the Ionians soul and body work together as a unity, the early Pythagoreans viewed the soul as alien to the body and contaminated in some way by it. Soul and body are in conflict, and human life is an enduring struggle between bodily pleasures and the purification of the soul. The *psuchē* is not corporeal but a 'number moving itself' (Plutarch, *Placita* 4.2). It has an independent existence, which survives after the death of the body by transmigrating into another one, of a different form.

The first extant fragment on transmigration is from Xenophanes and comes in an anecdote about Pythagoras quoted by Diogenes Laertius in the *Lives of Philosophers* (B7):

> They say that once, as he was passing by when a puppy was being beaten, he took pity on it, and spoke as follows: "Stop! don't hit it! for it is the soul of a friend of mine, which I recognised when I heard its voice."

The ironic tone of the passage could possibly suggest that the theory of transmigration was well known by Xenophanes' time. According to some later evidence (Diogenes Laertius 8.14.1–2; Porphyry, *Vita Pythagorae* 19), Pythagoras was the first philosopher to introduce the doctrine of transmigration into Greece.

The Pythagoreans believed in the transmigration of the soul, which follows the cyclic changes of bodily incarnations as plant, animal and human, with the possibility of entering a divine life. This theory echoes Orphic doctrines (Herodotus 2.18), according to which the body is the 'tomb' or 'prison' of the soul (Plato, *Cratylus* 400c). In Pythagorean eschatology the subjection of the soul to a different life-form happens according to one's present deeds, possibly only the 'noble' souls being released from the suffering of transmigration.

Alcmaeon of Croton also maintained that the soul is the divine source of life. It is a self-moving principle that attempts to imitate the perpetual circular motion of the heavenly bodies (A12); but, as Alcmaeon claimed, humans die because they cannot join the beginning with the end (B2).

Empedocles describes his own life as having taken many various forms – of humans, animals and even plants: "For before now I have been at some time boy and girl, bush, bird and a mute fish in the sea" (B117). This significant fragment for the early Greek concept of transmigration is frequently quoted in late authors. Its original meaning could be related, though not directly, to transmigration as a 'remembrance' of previous lives, but mainly to the 'decree' of the soul being born in different elements, which are treated as different kinds of lives. For Empedocles, the soul is a divine spirit (*daimōn*), which passes through a number of lives in different elements, represented as different kinds of mortal beings, by following the divine law of necessity (B115):

> There is a decree of necessity, ratified long ago by gods, eternal and sealed by broad oaths, that whenever anyone from fear defiles his own limbs in error, having mistakenly made false the oath he swore – *daimōnes* to whom life long-lasting is apportioned – he wanders from the blessed ones for three times ten thousand years, being born throughout the time as all kinds of

SOUL   57

mortal forms, exchanging one hard way of life for another. For the force of air pursues him into sea, and sea spits him out on to earth's surface, earth casts him into the rays of the blazing sun and sun into the eddies of air; one takes him from another and all abhor him. I too am now one of these, an exile from the gods and a wanderer, having put my trust in raging strife.

The fate of the *daimōnes* is ratified by an 'eternal oath,' which rules over the formation and separation of all mortal things. The *daimōnes* are not outside the 'decree of necessity,' so that their life is not perfect and immortal, but they are subject to the cosmic alterations of the four elements. The descent on earth is a decline, and the *daimōn* is portrayed as "clothed in an unfamiliar garment of flesh" (B126) and mortal creatures as "poor and unhappy," born out of strife and lamentation (B124). The bodily life in this world is limited in joy, pleasure and enlightenment by comparison to the life of gods: the life in the body is a "roofed cave" (B120). This metaphor perhaps anticipates Plato's allegory of humans living in a cave, in the *Republic* VII. However, even if Empedocles considers the soul as an "exile from the gods" (B115), he himself appears to enjoy the best human life as poet, prophet and healer (B112, B146, B147), as a person who has gained "the wealth of divine understanding," compared to one "who cherishes an unenlightened opinion about the gods" (B132).

6.3 Immortality and Time

The Presocratic reconsideration of the nature of soul and life brought a philosophical reaffirmation of the meaning of mortality and immortality, eternity and time at human, divine and cosmic level. Anaximander seems to be the first to introduce such a new perception of immortality. The recurring cosmological process of generation and destruction led him to the conclusion that all living beings have to be either mortal, with a beginning and end in time, or immortal, without such a beginning or end. The traditional notion of gods as having been born but having no death – like the endless life of the goddess Athena – should be considered unacceptable. Anaximander's conclusion reflects Xenophanes' later statement (reported by Aristotle at *Rhetoric* 1399^{b}5) that "those who say that the gods are born are as impious as those who say that they die" (A12). Anaximander's first principle is the *apeiron*, which is eternal, with no beginning or end, from which all things in the cosmos originate and return. Generation and destruction follow endlessly the cycles of mortal life, being controlled by the endless series of astronomical occurrences (A9, A11 and A12). Whereas order (*taxis*) gives the temporal limits of generation and destruction, the unlimited (*apeiron*) signifies eternity and lack of limitation (B1). Generation may be excessive and an 'unjust' action, for which compensation has to be paid under "the assessment of time" (*chronos*). Floods are balanced by droughts and hot summers by cold winters, in order to preserve a balanced equilibrium between the opposite forces of hot and cold, wet and dry, acting and reacting on each other with mutual gains and losses (B1).

Heraclitus relates immortality to the ever-living fire, and mortality to the flux of temporal becoming (B31). The ever-living fire is manifested in the three tensions of time – past, present and future – as having-been (past), being-now (present) and coming-to-be (future). Heraclitus' eternity (*aiōn*) is described as a divine child, a cosmic player, who controls the world's destiny with its own game (B52). Time is irreversible (B91): "it is not possible to step twice into the same river." Mortals cannot step in the same river as they cannot experience the same moment in life. "Over those who step into the same river ever different waters flow" (B12). As Plato states in the *Cratylus* (402a8–9), "all things are in flux and nothing stays still." The changes of the individual souls occur between the states of life and death that are named as the period of human time. The lifetime of any single being is defined by the condition of its soul and the limits of mortal life are between the limits of "living and dying, waking and sleeping, young and old" (B88).

For the Pythagoreans, time is "the soul of the universe" (Plutarch, *Quaestiones Platonicae* 8.4). Celestial motions mark the crucial periods of human life (Aristotle, *Metaphysics* 985[b] 30–37) and, because of the recurring cyclical movements of the planets within the pattern of a **Great Year**, the Pythagoreans supported the view that events on earth would follow the same turning of time-cycles, in endless recurrence. Eudemus drew the implications for his students (fr. 51, a text quoted by Simplicius, *In Aristotelis Physicorum libros commentaria* 732.26):

> **Great Year**
>
> the period of time during which all the planets return to the same configuration

If you believe what the Pythagoreans say, everything comes back in the same numerical order, and I shall deliver this lecture again to you with my staff in my hands as you sit there in the same way as now, and everything else shall be the same. It is also then reasonable to claim that time is the same, for if a movement is one and the same, then this will also be true of number, and of time as well.

On this basis, according to the Pythagorean Hippasus (A1), the periodic cycles of events in the cosmos are underlined by everlasting time, identified with the everlasting motion of the universe.

Despite the fact that Parmenides never referred to *psuchē* (at least not in the extant fragments of his poem), his account of eternity and time is worth mentioning. Parmenides denied the everlasting flux of temporal becoming and argued instead for an atemporal, unchanging immobility of being. Whereas Heraclitus supported an everlasting cosmos temporally divided into past, present and future, which always was, and is and will be (B30), Parmenides maintained the timelessness of being, which never was nor will be, since it is now (B8.5–6); 'what-is' is undivided in an atemporal present, without past or future. Parmenides argued that anything that is generated would necessarily presuppose a principle sufficient to explain its generation at a particular time. *Why would it start at one time rather than another?* Being cannot begin from not-being (B8.7–10) and, conversely, being cannot cease to be, since the existence of not-being has been rejected (B8.14). To become in time presupposes a prior state in the past (which is not now) and a posterior state in the future (which is not yet). However, since what-is-not has been rejected as impossible, past and future are impossible, and so what-is will never be extinguished or perish (B8.20–21).

For Empedocles, the lifetime of the *daimōnes* is a long-extended life between temporal life, which is related to humans, animals and plants, and eternal life, which is related to the four elements and to Love and Strife. All mortals are in an eternal cyclical exchange of position: from 'many' to 'one' and from 'one' to 'many' in different time periods (B17). The continuous repetition of the cosmic cycle signifies the ontological difference between the life of immortal elements and the life of mortal beings (B20–B22). The four 'immortal' roots are without temporal beginning or end; there is no addition or subtraction from the totality of being in the cosmos. Love and Strife are the eternal motivating forces that combine and separate the elements within the cosmic cycle. They have an everlasting life that always was and always will be – it is never going to be extinguished or exhausted in the future (B16): "They are as they were before and shall be, and never, I think, will everlasting life be emptied of these two." The continuous temporal exchange of mortal life during the mixing phase of Love and the separating phase of Strife makes it incompatible with and inferior to the 'everlasting abiding' of immortal life (B26). While mortals are subject to the temporality of becoming, the immortal elements and forces participate in the everlasting stability of being outside the alteration of coming-to-be and passing-away (B17.8–13).

Conclusion

The early Greek philosophers developed the concept of soul from the simple Homeric image of the *psuchē* as a flitting shade in Hades. The Presocratic *psuchē* is the source of life and of intelligence alike. It is an autonomous principle, which weaves together the microcosm of human life and intelligence with the macrocosm of the universe. Nevertheless, the Presocratics had different views on the actual nature of the soul. Thales thought of it as watery, Anaximenes as airy, connected with the breath of life, and Heraclitus as fiery, set against the destructive nature of water, while Leucippus and Democritus gave it an atomic structure. Alcmaeon and Philolaus placed the seat of consciousness and intelligence in the brain, and in this they were followed by Plato, whereas generally, in Greek psychology and medicine, the heart was the area thought to control life, emotion and intelligence. Anaxagoras maintained that *nous* is an active vital and intelligent force that regulates all living things endowed with *psuchē*; and here he was indebted to the *logos* of Heraclitus, which governs individuals as well as the whole cosmos. The early Pythagoreans found the soul to be in conflict with the body, and likely to be harmed by it. They therefore introduced transmigration as a significant factor in the relation of soul to body, giving an independent existence to soul, which continues after the death of the body and may transmigrate into another one, of a different form, according to the life previously led. Empedocles thought of the soul as being composed, like everything else, of the four elements, and he called it *daimōn:* as such, it might enjoy a long life, oscillating between eternity and time. Thus the Presocratic conception of the soul leads to a reaffirmation of the notions of time and immortality in relation to humans, gods and the cosmos.

Further Reading

Bremmer, J. (1983) *The Early Greek Concept of Soul*. Princeton University Press: Princeton.

Darcus, S. M. (1979) "A Person's Relation to ψυχή in Homer, Hesiod and the Greek Lyric Poets," *Glotta* 57: 30–39.

Gottschalk, H. P. (1971) "Soul as Harmonia," *Phronesis* 16: 179–198.

Hussey, E. (1991) "Heraclitus on Living and Dying," *The Monist* 74: 517–530.

Laks, A. (1999) "Soul, Sensation and Thought," in Long, A. A. (1999) *The Cambridge Companion to Early Greek Philosophy*. Cambridge: Cambridge University Press, 250–270.

Nussbaum, M. C. (1972) "ψυχή in Heraclitus," *Phronesis* 17: 1–16, 153–170.

Seligman, P. (1978) "Soul and Cosmos in Presocratic Philosophy," *Dionysius* 2: 5–17.

KNOWLEDGE

Introduction

Can we have genuine knowledge of the world? Can the human mind attain truth? Some Presocratics made a distinction between opinion (*doxa*) and truth (*alētheia*), relating the former to uncritical reasoning, the latter to critical doubt and careful reasoning. They also distinguished between knowing and believing, and they expressed a strong tendency towards skepticism – both in epistemic and in theological terms – often combined with pride in new discoveries, which represented genuine advances. For some Presocratics, true knowledge is possible trough careful observation and valid argumentation. The wise is able to recognize the true nature of things behind the perceptible phenomena. However, progress from ignorance to knowledge would come not from amassing and assembling facts (*polumathia*), but from investigation (*historia*) and working things out (*logos*), in open criticism and counter-criticism of human knowledge and of our commonly held views about the gods.

Introduction to Presocratics: A Thematic Approach to Early Greek Philosophy with Key Readings, First Edition. Giannis Stamatellos.
© 2012 John Wiley & Sons, Inc. Published 2012 by John Wiley & Sons, Inc.

7.1 Doubting the Gods

Xenophanes criticized polytheism and the anthropomorphic descriptions of the Olympian deities. Humans erroneously suppose that their gods have human characteristics (B14). The image of the gods, as humans portray them, is always relative to the region and culture in which it is expressed (B16): "Ethiopians say that their gods are snubnosed and black, and Thracians that theirs have blue eyes and red hair." The subjectivity of our cognition leads us humans to suppose that gods have been born, or that they have a human voice and body (B15):

> But if <horses> or cows or lions had hands to draw with and produce works of art as humans do, horses would draw the figures of gods like horses and cows like cows, and in each case they would make their bodies just in the form they themselves have.

Xenophanes proposed to substitute for the old anthropomorphic polytheism the concept of 'one god' – an intelligent and superior deity beyond any human or physical description (B23): "One god, greatest among gods and men, not at all like mortals in body or mind." Xenophanes' god is all-seeing, all-thinking and all-hearing, with a complete perception of the world (B24): "As a whole he sees, as a whole he thinks and as a whole he hears." The one god is motionless – (B26): "always he stays in the same place, not moving at all, nor is it fitting for him to travel in different directions at different times" – but he is the cause of movement: "with no effort at all he keeps everything moving by the thinking of his mind" (B25). This suggestion – of a single, intelligent, powerful and omnipresent god, who "keeps everything moving" –reinterprets traditional polytheism, which attributed to individual gods natural phenomena such as earthquakes, volcanoes and rainbows.

Empedocles also criticized and rejected anthropomorphic accounts of the gods and replaced them with that of a single, non-anthropomorphic god (B134):

> He is not equipped with a human head on a body, two branches do not spring from his back, he has no feet, no swift knees, no shaggy genitals, but he is mind alone, holy and inexpressible, darting through the whole cosmos with swift thoughts.

The god of Empedocles, like the god of Xenophanes, is an intelligent deity: a *holy mind*. At the stage of the cycle dominated by Love, this god is described as a rounded sphere rejoicing in encircling stillness, equal to itself in every direction, without any temporal or spatial differentiation (B27–B29). For Empedocles, the new gods are the four immortal elements, given divine names that may indicate their everlasting power and supremacy (B6).

The early atomists also discarded the traditional concept of divinity. In their atomic theory, the gods we seem to be familiar with are "idols of the mind" (B166), merely effluences from divine beings; they live far away in the spaces between world systems, untroubled by human affairs. However, as Leucippus asserts in the only extant fragment from his work *On Mind* (B2), we should consider that "nothing occurs at random but everything for a reason and by necessity." Atomic necessity (*anankē*) is related to the pre-cosmic initial motion of atoms in void and describes the *non-planned* sequence of physical events *contra* divine intervention. Every event in this world is the result of a chain of atomic collisions, actions and reactions.

7.2   Human Knowledge

Xenophanes had been skeptical about human knowledge and widespread views about the world. He gave the example of people speaking of the rainbow as the goddess Iris, when it is only a particular cloud formation (B32): "and the one they call Iris – even this is by nature a cloud, purple and crimson and yellow to see." Anaxagoras' later assertion "we call Iris the light in the clouds facing the sun" (B19) probably recalls Xenophanes' criticism. Moreover, for Xenophanes, humans base their views on relative, predetermined conditions: "if god had not made yellow honey, people would say that figs are much sweeter" (B38). Xenophanes is self-critical; he is aware that even his own views are only an assumption: "opinion is stretched over all" (B34):

> And so no man has seen anything clearly nor will there be anyone who knows about the gods and about what I say on everything; for if one should by chance speak about what has come to pass even as it is, still he himself does not know, but opinion is stretched over all.

Knowledge about the divine and everything else is inaccessible to us, and even if we chanced on the truth we would not recognize it as such. However, time is an important factor, which improves our discoveries and brings us closer to knowledge (B18): "gods of course did not reveal everything to mortals from the beginning, but in time, by searching, they improve their discoveries."

Parmenides criticized human knowledge arising from sense-perception. Humans are misled by their senses into supposing that there are many existing things, which are born and die and change. In the account of human opinions, it is said that the constituent proportions of 'light' and 'night' might distinguish perceptible things (B9): "Since all things have been named light and night, and the names which belong to the powers of each have been assigned, all is full at once of light and of dark night, both equal, since nothing is without either." In this context, 'names' are not arbitrary connections between words and objects, but they reflect the different proportions of light and night in perceptible things. The proportion of light and night in the physical constitution of the perceiver also determines the nature of thinking (B16).

Melissus followed Parmenides' criticism of sense-perception. Since our senses record constant change and yet change is logically impossible, the sensible observations and data are untrustworthy. Since what is really existent is one and unchangeable and the senses seem to be aware of many things, perception, again, is at odds with the single and unique existence of being, and hence it is unreliable. There is no plurality in reality (B8):

> If there were many things they would have to be such as I say the one is. For if there are earth and water and air and fire and iron and gold, and one living and another dead, and again black and white and all the other things that people say are true and real, if indeed these things exist and we see and hear them correctly, each must be such as it seemed to us at first, and they cannot change or become different, but each is always as it is.

Therefore, since plurality has to be denied and being is one, single and undivided, any perception of change and differentiation remains unjustified.

Anaxagoras agreed with other Presocratics that the senses could deceive us (A96). As he illustrated in a famous example, snow is not white, as the senses present it; for, since snow is frozen water and water is black, snow must also be black (A97). Anaxagoras attempted to explain sensation by appealing to the principle of perception through unlikes (A92). *Contra* Empedocles' principle (which probably originated with Parmenides) that *like is perceived by like* – as expressed in B109:

"with earth we perceive earth, with water water, with air divine air, with fire destructive fire, with love love, and strife with baneful strife" – Anaxagoras claimed *that unlike is perceived by unlike*. Anaxagoras explained that all perception is a kind of distress, and stronger stimuli such as bright colors and loud noises cause an irritating pain in the perceiving sense organ (A92 and A94). Sense perception occurs through perceptible impressions that are opposite (A92): in touch and taste especially, the opposite is recognized by the opposite, as hot is to the touch of a cold hand, or sweet after a bitter taste. However, due to the restricted range of their senses, humans are unable "to judge the truth" (B21), and so what is seen gives only a glimpse of the unseen (B21a); yet even the least observable 'glimpse' of reality could lead some humans to understand the truth of things through the interrelation of human mind to the universal *nous* (B12).

Democritus, like Heraclitus, Parmenides and Empedocles, offered a contrast between reason and the senses. He spoke of two sorts of knowledge: genuine and obscure. Whereas obscure knowledge refers to sense perception, genuine knowledge refers to reasoning as the only way of recognizing the presence of atoms in the shadow of appearances (B11) – the atoms are too small to be in the range of sight, hearing or touch. Even so, definite knowledge is practically unobtainable: "in reality we know nothing; for truth is in the depths" (B117). Objective knowledge of the world, in terms of a direct correspondence of the human senses to reality, is not possible, and, since human understanding alters with the disposition of atoms, the nature of any individual object is perplexing (B8); however, conscious efforts can improve our progress from ignorance to understanding (B241). It would be more appropriate to speak about a subjective perception of reality, insofar as the effluence of a sensible object reflects its nature on the senses (B7). Our understanding shifts in accordance with the disposition of the body and of the things that enter it, as well as of those that push against it.

In particular, for Democritus, perception results from the out-flowing of atoms of the perceived object, which connect with the relevant sense organs; and the apparent qualities of this object exist only by convention (B9):

> By convention sweet and bitter, by convention hot and cold, by convention colour, but in reality atoms and void. [...] In reality we know nothing for certain, but there is change according to the condition of the body and of what enters it and comes up against it.

Hence Democritus made a further distinction between appearance and reality. In reality only atoms and void exist, and the perceptible world is just a compound of atoms and void (B9). A structure of atoms, too small to be seen, lies behind the world of everyday experience, and the perception of qualities is merely a matter of convention. Size and shape are given as primary qualities of atoms, while color, taste and other apparent qualities are secondary qualities resulting from the various shapes, movements and positions of the atoms. This means that, since only atoms and void exist in reality and our senses do not have direct access to this reality, no accurate knowledge is possible through the senses (B7). But we do have to start from them, as Democritus vividly describes in a personification of the senses (B125): "wretched mind – after getting your evidence from us, you throw us down; but the throw brings you down with us."

7.3 Truth and Wisdom

For some Presocratics, true knowledge is not unattainable. The Milesian thinkers attempted to explain perceptible reality and the cosmos through sense experience and valid inference. Thales (A14) and Anaximenes (B2) seem to have relied on the fact that, if two things have certain properties in common at a small scale, they should have the same properties in common at a large scale. For example, Thales suggested that, just as a piece of wood floats on a pond (= small scale), so the earth floats on water (= large scale). Careful observation of phenomena and analogical reasoning could lead us to some understanding both of individual objects and of the world as a whole.

Heraclitus also accepted the power of the senses (B55: "All that is seen and heard and learnt I honour above all"; see also B101a). However, he maintained that the senses alone are not helpful for those who have 'barbarian souls' and do not understand the real constitution of things (B107). Many people do not really know how to listen or speak (B19), and the ability to learn many things or to assemble facts (*polumathia*) is not sufficient to a genuine understanding of the world (B40). The right path is to grasp the hidden *logos* of nature, which moves and regulates all things; we have to understand how the *logos* "steers everything through everything" (B41). However, although all things happen according to the *logos* (B1) and thinking is common to all (B113), people generally behave as 'deaf hearers' (B34), 'asleep' in their ignorance (B1). Although the *logos* is common, "most people live as if they had a private under-standing of their own" (B2). Those who are aware of the universality of the *logos* are able to recognize that the cosmos is one and common to all (B89). Heraclitus admits to his own limitation of language: "listening not to me but to the *logos*, it is wise to agree that one is all and all is one" (B50). The *logos* is the one and only 'wise' entity (B32); it is the unifying principle that simplifies what is apparently complex and contradictory.

The early Pythagoreans believed that truth could be found in the knowledge of mathematics. Philolaus of Croton connected knowledge with numbers, going as far as to say that it is impossible to know anything without reference to numbers (B4). All things that are known have a mathematical basis, and 'number' is a necessary prerequisite of knowl-edge (B4). True knowledge of the universe is derived from the under-standing of its mathematical structure and connections, and, if there was not this structure but all things were unlimited, knowledge would be impossible (B3): "there would not be any recognizable first principle, if everything is unlimited."

Parmenides argued that truth should be established through the onto-logical correlation between thinking and being. It is impossible to accept what-is-not, and so, if thinking takes place, it follows that something has *to be* in order to be recognized and understood (B2 and B6). Since *what-is* alone can be apprehended by thinking, "what can be thought of is the same as what can be" (B3). That it is impossible to find thought without being is reiterated in the longer stretch of argument (B8.34–36): "What is there to be thought of is the same as what is thought, for you will not find thinking apart from what-is, which is what is referred to." What-is reveals itself in the constant contemplation of the mind (B4): "Contemplate steadily what is absent as present to your mind; for it will never cut off what is from holding to what it is, since it neither scatters in every direction in every away nor draws together in order."

For Empedocles, truth is difficult and learning is hard (B114). Human powers are constricted, and, due to many distractions, we come to the wrong conclusions in a limited lifetime (B2). However, with the author-ity and inspiration of the Muse (B3, B23.11), humans may begin attain-ing knowledge themselves (B4): "It is indeed the habit of the mischievous to distrust authority, but learn yourself as the assurances of my Muse urge, once the argument has been articulated within your breast." Learning increases wisdom (B17.13), and thinking is in the heart blood (B105). With Empedocles as guide we should push his words, and the thoughts contained in them, down into the heart and not be distracted (B110). Empedocles tells us that we have to start from what is obvious, since wisdom "grows according to what is present" (B106). Knowledge comes from recognizing the four roots in the first place – fire/sun, air, earth and water, which are all around us – and understanding how they are united by the power of Love (B71). The presence and effects of joy and love are acknowledged within us (B17.27), and Love and Strife are well known around us (B20.1). We are familiar with the power of Love to bring things together, although we cannot literally see it (B17.25). "It is not possible to bring <the divine> close within reach of our eyes or to grasp it with the hands, by which the broadest path of persuasion for men leads to the mind" (B133). Gaining understanding is the best human activity, and someone who, like Pythagoras (B129), has gained the "wealth of divine understanding" is happy in his wisdom (B132). Wise people such as prophets, poets, doctors or statesmen rise at the level of honored gods (B146): "At the end they come on earth among men as prophets, minstrels, physicians and leaders, and from these they arise as gods, highest in honour." In so doing the wise transcend human sorrows and distress (B147).

Conclusion

The Presocratic thinkers were the first to make a clear distinction between opinion and truth. Whereas opinion is based on uncritical acceptance of commonly held views, truth is based on careful reasoning arising from critical doubt. Such doubt was prevalent in the Presocratic re-evaluation of the nature of human knowledge and embedded traditions concerning the world and the gods. Xenophanes and Empedocles criticized the anthropomorphic gods of Greek religion and in their place proposed a non-anthropomorphic intelligent deity, involved in cosmic processes. The early atomists also denied the traditional gods as 'idols of the mind.' Most of the Presocratics stressed the unreliability of the human senses; and, because our senses may deceive us, sense perception is to be rejected as a means of understanding basic truths. Traditional teaching may also be based on relative, subjective and predetermined criteria and conditions, and

(Continued)

polumathia, erudition, with its learned assembling of facts, is no guide to wisdom. Hence Parmenides and Empedocles emphasized the power of thinking and argument over seeing and hearing as reliable ways of making progress towards the truth, and Democritus in particular distinguished between obscure knowledge, based on the senses, and genuine knowledge, derived from valid reasoning. Thales and Anaximenes introduced careful observation and an analogical form of reasoning into their explanations of the world. Heraclitus recognized the usefulness of the senses as guides to understanding, while emphasizing that true knowledge is only possible through awareness of the universality of the wisdom of the *logos*. The Pythagoreans took a different approach, by connecting knowledge to mathematical reasoning. Since everything known was thought to have a mathematical basis, knowledge of numbers and of their interconnection is a necessary prerequisite to true knowledge. Parmenides further argued that truth can be established through thinking about what really *is*. The ontological correlation between thinking and being leads to an epistemic justification of truth. Empedocles similarly recognized that human powers are restricted, and encouraged the attainment of knowledge through conscious effort and hard learning.

Further Reading

Broadie, S. (1999) "Rational Theology," in Long (ed.), 205–224.

Curd, P. K. (1991) "Knowledge and Unity in Heraclitus," *The Monist* 74: 531–549.

Fränkel, H. (1974) "Xenophanes' Empiricism and His Critique of Knowledge (B34)," in Mourelatos (ed.), 118–131.

Hussey, E. (1982) "Epistemology and Meaning in Heraclitus," in Schofield and Nussbaum (eds.), 1–32.

Hussey, E. (1990) "The Beginnings of Epistemology: From Homer to Philolaos," in Everson, S. (ed.), *Epistemology*, Cambridge: Cambridge University Press, 11–38.

Lesher, J. H. (1999) "Early Interest in Knowledge," in Long (ed.), 225–249.

Lesher, J. H. (2008) "The Humanizing Knowledge in Presocratic Thought," in Curd and Graham (eds.), 458–484.

Pachenko, D. (1993) "Thales and the Origin of Theoretical Reasoning," *Configurations* 3: 387–484.

Robinson, T. M. (2008) "Presocratic Theology," in Curd and Graham, 485–498.

8

ETHICS

Introduction

Aristotle regarded Socrates as the philosopher who wondered extensively about "ethical matters" (*Metaphysics* 987^{b}2). He maintained that Socrates' teaching focused on definitions, found not in the world of nature as a whole, but in the universal principles of ethics. Cicero (106–43 BCE) also declared that "Socrates was the first who brought down philosophy from heaven to earth and placed it in cities, and introduced it even in homes, and drove it to inquire about life and customs and things good and evil" (*Tusculan Disputations* V.10). However, the extant fragments of the major Presocratics demonstrate a wide range of topics, including subjects of moral significance. The Presocratics were not only concerned with the structure of the cosmos and the basic principles of physical reality, but they were also involved in a discussion on moral excellence and the importance of human values — what we term 'virtue ethics.'

Introduction to Presocratics: A Thematic Approach to Early Greek Philosophy with Key Readings, First Edition. Giannis Stamatellos.
© 2012 John Wiley & Sons, Inc. Published 2012 by John Wiley & Sons, Inc.

8.1   Heroic Ethics

Homeric heroes portrayed the moral ideal of human excellence. In the heroic societies of what may roughly be termed 'the Homeric era' – that is, the world depicted in the Homeric poems – virtue (*aretē*) was used for excellence of any kind. In the *Iliad* a fast runner has the *aretē* of his feet (20.411), and an excellent son displays the *aretē* of his mind and physical strength (15.642). The *Iliad* and the *Odyssey* describe two different heroic figures: Achilles in the *Iliad* is the most excellent in battle and when it comes to being passionate, while Odysseus in the *Odyssey* is the most excellent in being cunning and patient. Achilles and Odysseus are the heroic images that represent the dominant agonistic paradigms in Greek culture. Excellence in virtue is applicable both at a personal and at a social level. For example, excellence in courage is a dominant and central virtue that defines the quality or power of an individual to sustain both a household and a community. The individual who is brave in battle is rewarded with everlasting glory. Being **agathos** was also a question of class; whereas outstanding warriors were noble and virtuous, the **kakos** was weak and of low birth. Then the Homeric heroes were subject to divine favor too – or interference from the gods. Achilles was under the protection of Athena, while Odysseus constantly faced the anger of Poseidon.

> **agathos**
>
> good, brave, virtuous

> **kakos**
>
> bad or evil (denotes the absence of good)

In Hesiod's *Works and Days* the virtuous man is the one who acts in accordance with justice. While in Homer the hero's *aretē* is to excel, in Hesiod it is not to exceed. Whereas Homeric *aretē* refers to self-assertion, Hesiodic *aretē* is related to self-control. The latter is encapsulated in the Delphic exhortation *mēden agan*, "nothing too much," and underlies the moral frame of early Greek philosophical ethics. In the same spirit, according to some ancient sources, Thales seems to have introduced the saying *gnōthi sauton*, "know yourself" (A1 and A2), which supplements the Delphic moral exhortation for moderation and associates Presocratic philosophy with self-knowledge and self-control. Thales' pupil Anaximander further correlates the well-ordered *cosmos* with the well-ordered *polis*: in the city state as in the natural world, excess and injustice bring retribution (B1).

However, some Presocratics were critical of the immoral spirit of epic poetry; thus Heraclitus of Ephesus criticized Homer and Hesiod (B42 and B57). And yet Xenophanes of Colophon seems to be the first philosopher to have raised strong, serious arguments against Homer's and Hesiod's immoral epics; after him Plato did the same in the *Republic* (377d ff.). Xenophanes wrote didactic and satiric poetry criticizing the epic tradition on the grounds that it ascribes to the gods unlawful actions such as deception, theft and adultery. Homeric epics portrayed the gods as immoral, unjust and unlawful (B11): "Homer and Hesiod have attributed to the gods everything that is blameworthy and disgraceful among humans – theft and adultery and mutual trickery."

The reason behind Xenophanes' criticism should be found in his own poetry, and also in his position as a poet. Xenophanes adopted the traditional view of the poet as a divinely inspired moral educator. On this model, the poet is the mortal who, with inspiration from the Muses, stands between the gods and the human world. Xenophanes also wanted to fortify epic poetry against any attack from the emerging philosophical prose of the Ionians. This kind of poetry also had didactic power, which made it important as a form of rational expression and of moral teaching. The divinely inspired poet is closer to the gods; from this privileged position he is able to express the true morality of the gods and to reveal divine knowledge. Whereas Xenophanes recognizes his own limitation as a philosopher (B34), he wants also to emphasize the authority of the poet as the best possible provider of divine wisdom and morality. The poet is able to reveal divine knowledge despite human ignorance, subjectivity and relativity.

Empedocles' didactic poetry reflected that of Xenophanes, but more particularly it promoted, among the citizens of Acragas, a specific frame of mind in thinking about natural morality (B112, B114). Humans and animals have a similar physical structure, living in the same cosmos and getting involved in the same struggle for life and survival (B115, B117). The ontological relationship between various kinds of beings in the world justifies respect and friendship between us and the others (B130).

8.2 Virtue Ethics

> **virtue ethics**
>
> a character-based ethical approach, which focuses on the quality or virtue of the moral agent rather than on the duties or the consequences of the moral action

Virtue ethics is originally associated with Socratic moral teaching. For Socrates, the most important task in human life is the care of the soul – the intellectual and the moral self of every human being. Socrates maintained that an unexamined life is not worth living. Knowledge is preferable to ignorance, and the knowledge of virtue stands above all. Knowledge itself is virtue, and to know how to behave and act towards the good should be the most fundamental aim of human life. Socrates' virtue ethics is reflected in Plato's eudemonistic ethics, based on the soul's pure contemplation of the Forms. The Platonic cardinal virtues of wisdom, justice, self-control and courage (as presented in the *Symposium*, the *Phaedo*, the *Pheadrus* and the *Republic*) are related to human excellence. Aristotle develops virtue ethics theory even further, in the *Nicomachean Ethics* and in the *Eudemian Ethics*. He considers ethics as a form of practical philosophy dealing with the character and behavior of the individual in the community. For Aristotle, the purpose (*telos*) of human life is happiness (*eudaimonia*) achieved through virtue or excellence – that is, a disposition concerning choice that is grounded in **moderation**. A moral agent is not good and happy only by choosing the right action, but also by knowing the right way to do it.

> **moderation**
>
> in Aristotle, a mean between the two extremes of deficiency and excess

However, whereas virtue ethics developed, and was extensively discussed, in the classical age, the Presocratic philosophical tradition should not be excluded from an inquiry into the nature of virtue at an earlier age. Heraclitus emphasized human *ēthos* (B119): "a person's character [*ēthos*] is his destiny." Our destiny, that is, what happens to us, can be attributed to our *ēthos*, which results from the habit of certain kinds of actions and thoughts that affect the physical composition of the soul. Heraclitus introduces a new heroic quality. Humans determine their destiny; in this way prudence and wisdom become significant virtues of human life. All humans "are able to know themselves and be prudent" (B116), and to be prudent is the "greatest virtue" (B112): "The greatest virtue is to be prudent [*phronein*], and wisdom is to speak the truth and to act with understanding according to nature." To be prudent, to think soundly in accordance to the *logos*, is to maintain and control opposite tensions in a harmonious balance. The wisdom of the *logos* is applied to the structure and functioning of both the *cosmos* and the *polis*. Thus the human law (*nomos*) that unites the *polis* should follow the one divine law (*logos*) that binds the cosmos (B114):

> Those who speak with sense must rely on what is common to all, as a city must rely on its law, and with much greater reliance; for all the human

laws are nourished by one divine law; for it has as much power as it wishes and is sufficient for all and is still not exhausted.

The citizens must be politically active: they have to "fight for the law as for their city wall" (B44).

Heraclitus' ethics is linked to his physics and psychology. Fire constitutes the living bodies and the cosmos in physical terms; human *ēthos* and wisdom, in psychological terms. Wise men have souls close to the natural proportions of fire and *logos*, and only the fiery soul reflects wisdom and *logos*. When the soul fails to control its *thumos* (B85) and indulges its desires and anger, it loses its fiery substance and becomes 'wet.' Whereas the soul is 'delighted' to be wet (B77), the 'wet soul' is that of a drunken man led stumbling along by a boy (B117); it is the soul of a man who lost control over body movements and speech. The soul that is closer to fire – the 'dry soul' – is the wisest and the best (B118). The 'dry soul' is the 'best soul,' and "the best choose one thing above all: everlasting fame among men; but most gorge themselves like cattle" (B29). Heraclitus also stresses the danger of insolence: *hubris* should be put out more firmly than a fire (B43). It is difficult to control the desires of the soul: "it is hard to fight against impulse; whatever it wants, it buys at the expense of the soul" (B85), and sometimes "it is not better for people to get what they want" (B110).

However, for Heraclitus, to be *aristos* (best) is not an easy task: "one man is as ten thousand, if he is the best" (B49). Hence Heraclitus emphasizes the importance of the Delphic exhortation for self-knowledge with the statement "I searched myself" (B101). Self-knowledge is a prerequisite for true wisdom and for the understanding of *logos*. The best soul recognizes the hidden *logos* that underlies the phenomena (B1) and the *logos* that lies in the depths of the soul (B45): "you could not in your going find the limits of soul though you travelled the whole way – so deep is its *logos*."

Pythagorean ethics is related to the purification of the soul. According to Diogenes Laertius (*Lives of Philosophers* 8.65 f.), Pythagoreans seems to have asserted that "virtue is harmony," particularly related to health, goodness and god himself. Plato (*Republic* 600b) testifies to the fact that Pythagoras instituted a recommended way of life (*bios*) known as 'the Pythagorean *bios*.' The virtuous soul purifies itself though music, mathematics and an appropriate diet. The laws of harmony underlie human relationships, bodily life and the cosmos. Moreover, according to Neoplatonic evidence, Pythagorean ethics was conducted practically, through oral maxims or aphorisms known as **akousmata**. As Iamblichus reports (*De vita Pythagorica* 82), the Pythagorean *akousmata* were divided

> **akousmata**
>
> things heard; oral aphorisms/ instructions of the Pythagoreans

into three categories, according to (1) "what a thing is"; (2) "what is the most important"; and (3) "what one must do or not do." The *akousmata* constituted a kind of proverbial wisdom; the corpus contained advice such as "pluck not

the crown," "eat not heart," or "when on a journey, turn not back" (Porphyry, *De vita Pythagorae* 42).

Empedocles followed Heraclitus in regarding human *ēthos* as determined by physical structure and habitual behavior. The wise man is the one who recognizes the true words that advance thought and understanding (B110). Empedocles urges Pausanias to listen carefully to the words that have been said on the psychical constitution of things, put them "into the heart" and reflect and contemplate on them throughout life (B110):

> If you push them firmly under your crowded thoughts, and contemplate them favourably with unsullied and constant attention, assuredly all these will be with you through life, and you will gain much else from them, for of themselves they will cause each thing to grow into the character, according to the nature of each. But if you yourself shall reach out for the countless trivialities which come among men and dull their meditations, straightaway these will leave you as the time comes round, longing to reach their own familiar kind; for know that all things have consciousness and a share of intelligence.

Empedocles claimed that the advanced thinking that humans are capable of is explained by the proportionate mixture of elements in the blood around the heart (B105). Thus human beings can improve their understanding and, consequently, their moral outlook through their own efforts, especially by allowing the philosopher's teaching to grow into their character. Humans are able to improve the quality of their life and thought through constant attention and effort; and they are responsible for it, too.

> **phronēsis**
>
> practical wisdom (*phronein* = to be prudent)

Empedocles (B117) considered himself to be an *ego* – or self – who attained the highest form of earthly life by achieving **phronēsis**; and this he did through the best possible mixture of the four elements. He held that thinking is determined by the body's elements, but that the consequent predispositions can be countered by teaching, motivation and effort. The external condition affects the internal structure (B106: "human wisdom grows according to what is present"), but an internal change of structure results in a change of thought (B108: "insofar as they have changed in their nature, so far changed thoughts are always present to them"). Nevertheless, Empedocles knows that 'listening' to the truth is a difficult task: "my friends, I know that there is truth in the words which I shall speak, but it is very difficult for men, and the onrush of conviction to the mind is unwelcome" (B114).

8.3 Atomic Ethics

Democritus followed Heraclitus and Empedocles in claiming that physical structure correlates and interacts with psychical structure. The coherence of the soul's structure is established through a certain *bios*, a recommended way of life, as in the case of Pythagoras. Despite the fact that Democritus is well known for his atomic theory and that atomism, with its rejection of teleology, would not tie in with the cultivation of moral virtue according to the ancient philosophers themselves, his ethical theory should not be dismissed. Most of his 160 extant fragments dealing with ethics come from two collections: the one compiled by Stobaeus (*Florilegium*) and the *Sayings of Democrates*. The two collections have 30 fragments in common, and Stobaeus is occasionally supported by other doxographers. Moreover, the list of works by Democritus reported by Diogenes Laertius (9.37) includes writings on physics, mathematics, medicine, music, agriculture and ethics, which is the basis for his reputation as the *pentathlos* of philosophy. These subjects could belong to the same philosophical corpus.

Democritus seems to be the first Presocratic to offer a comprehensive ethical work: *Peri euthumias* (*On Serenity*). This work covered a wide range of ethical issues such as fortune, prudence, pleasure, favors, friendship, punishment and child-caring. Democritus' moral inquiry is related to psychological motives for right conduct through knowledge, responsibility and self-respect (B181: "by doing right from understanding and knowledge one becomes simultaneously brave and straight-thinking"). According to Diogenes Laertius, for Democritus (A1) the aim is serenity, which is not the same as pleasure, as some have mistakenly supposed, but a calm and stable state of soul, in which it is not disturbed by any fear or superstition or any other emotion. He also calls it "well-being" and by many other names.

Humans attain serenity through enjoyment and the avoidance of extremes (B191: "serenity comes to people from moderation in pleasure and harmony in life"). Appropriate choices establish habits over time that lessen the force of the external impacts on the soul. It is best for a man to live his life as serenely as possible and with the least distress (B189). Appropriate habits minimize the internal disturbances of the soul and strengthen the coherence of its structure.

Moreover, for Democritus, nature and teaching are similar in that they both have an informative and reformative power. (B33): "nature and teaching are similar, for teaching re-forms the individual, and in re-forming establishes his nature." Continuous effort, practice and education establish the appropriate virtues as patterns of behavior and intellectual rigor (B182). Happiness is of the soul (B170) and, since the *psuchē* is rational, happiness is based on reason and not related to bodily satisfaction. For example, courage is not a result of an irrational emotive tendency, but the outcome of reason, knowledge and wisdom (B181). The gifts of wisdom 're-form' the soul (B197), and bring it to its *telos*, which is the main atomic quasi-virtue of serenity (A1). *Euthumia* is the *telos*, and "untroubled wisdom is worth everything, being most honoured" (B126). Thus the wise man is not just the citizen of a single *polis* but also the citizen of the whole world: "the wise man can walk the whole earth, for the entire cosmos is the homeland of the good soul" (B247).

Conclusion

An interest in virtue and in the excellence of human character belongs not only to the Socratic and immediately post-Socratic movements but can be traced back to early Greek philosophy and even further, to the epic poetry of Homer and Hesiod, which involved in its subject matter moral excellence and the significance of human values. The use of such terms such as *ēthos* and *aretē* by the Presocratics bridged the worlds of epic heroism and classical moral philosophy.

Presocratic ethics was distinctive in being generally linked to physics and psychology. Heraclitus, for example, stressed the psychological origins of human morality in a physical state, namely the fiery state of the soul; the Pythagoreans related ethics to harmony and purification; while Empedocles claimed that human *ēthos* is determined by elemental structures and improved by correct habitual behavior. Democritus seems to be the first to offer a complete ethical discussion on the advantage of serenity (*euthumia*) as both avoidance of extremes and positive enjoyment. He introduced a form of atomic ethics by correlating atomic structures at a physical and psychic level and by finding a means of enhancing the quality of life through personal, internal effort and the external influence of education. Early Greek inquiries into moral questions show that philosophical ethics, particularly in relation to individual human life and the society of citizens, was consciously discussed and elaborated upon in the Presocratic tradition.

Further Reading

Darcus, S. (1974) "Daimon as a Force Shaping Ethos in Heraclitus," *Phoenix* 28: 390–407.

Engman, J. (1991) "Cosmic Justice in Anaximander," *Phronesis* 36: 1–25.

Huby, P. (1967) *Greek Ethics*. London: Macmillan.

Kahn, C. H. (2003) "Presocratic Greek Ethics," in L. C. Becker and C. B. Becker, (eds.), *A History of Western Ethics*, Routledge, 1–8.

Vlastos, G. (1975) "Ethics and Physics in Democritus," in Allen and Furley (eds.), 381–408.

9

CONCLUSION

The Presocratic philosophers moved from mythology to rational think-ing as they explored the forces and principles that underlie human life and the natural world. Their approach, rather than being naïve and of mere historical interest, should be regarded as an innovative inquiry into fundamental questions of philosophy. Despite the fragmentary nature of the direct evidence, the early Greek accounts reveal the characteristics of argument and debate, bold theory and the initiation of self-reflection on the processes of learning and knowing. They present a discourse concerned with being and the cosmos, the primary stuff of the universe, the structure and function of the human soul, and the underlying principles governing perceptible phenomena, human knowledge and morality.

The Presocratic thinkers were particularly interested in the primary material and formal principles from which the world originates and on the basis of which it is structured as an ordered whole. This study involved an in-depth discussion of being and becoming in the context of the ontological status of the cosmos. Eternity and time were also discussed in relation to life and existence. The human soul was explained as an independent and sometimes eternal principle of life and intelli-gence, a principle functioning both at a human and cosmic level. The skepticism, common to many early Greek philosophers, toward tradi-

Introduction to Presocratics: A Thematic Approach to Early Greek Philosophy with Key Readings, First Edition. Giannis Stamatellos.
© 2012 John Wiley & Sons, Inc. Published 2012 by John Wiley & Sons, Inc.

tional views of the world and of the gods led to a reconsideration of the nature of divinity, of human knowledge and of the reliability of the senses. Progress towards truth was thought to be possible through critical thinking, conscious effort, education and constant contemplation of the world. A discourse on human morality brought with it a discussion of human character, values and virtues, which was later relevant to Socratic and post-Socratic philosophical ethics.

The variety of Presocratic theories reveals a fine and detailed philosophical exploration of issues that were further developed in subsequent traditions. Later thinkers discovered and interpreted the Presocratics – individually or as a group – in different ways and using different approaches, so that the impact of early Greek philosophy can be traced in a variety of disciplines, including mathematics, natural sciences and ethics.

Appendix A

Translation of the Main Fragments
M. R. Wright

Thales of Miletus

1 (A12)   There always has to be some natural substance, one or more than one, which endures while the rest are generated from it. They do not however all agree on the number and character of such a principle. Thales, the founder of this type of philosophy, says that the first principle is water (and that is why he claimed that the earth rests on water), perhaps having reached this conclusion from observing that nourishment is universally moist, and that even heat is generated from moisture and fuelled by it [...] That is why he reached this conclusion, and also because seed generally has a moist character and water is the principle of what has the natural character of being moist. *Aristotle*

2 (A22)   Thales thought that all things are full of gods. *Aristotle*

Anaximander of Miletus

1 (B1)   From the source from which they arise, to that they return of necessity when they are destroyed, "for they suffer punishment and make reparation to one another for their injustice according to the assessment of time," as he says in somewhat poetical terms. *Simplicius*

Introduction to Presocratics: A Thematic Approach to Early Greek Philosophy with Key Readings, First Edition. Giannis Stamatellos.
© 2012 John Wiley & Sons, Inc. Published 2012 by John Wiley & Sons, Inc.

2 (A11)   He said that the *archē* [beginning and basis] of existing things is an *apeiron* [limitless] nature of some kind, from which come the heavens and the *kosmos* [world order] in them. *Hippolytus*

3 (B3)   <the indefinite> deathless and indestructible [...] *Aristotle*

4 (B5)   He compared the earth to <a section of > a stone column. *Aetius*

Anaximenes of Miletus

1 (A5)   Anaximenes, Anaximander's colleague, agreed with him that there was one underlying nature, but not, as he said, that it was limitless but limited, naming it as air; and by thinning and thickening it makes individual objects different. *Simplicius*

2 (B2)   As our soul, which is air, maintains us, so breath and air surround the whole world. *Aetius*

3 (B2a)   The sun is broad and flat, like a leaf. *Aetius*

Xenophanes of Colophon

10 (B11)   Homer and Hesiod have attributed to the gods everything that is blameworthy and disgraceful among humans – theft and adultery and mutual trickery. *Sextus*

11 (B14)   [H]umans suppose that gods have been born, and wear clothes like theirs and have voice and body. *Clement*

12 (B15)   But if <horses> or cows or lions had hands to draw with and produce works of art as humans do, horses would draw the figures of gods like horses and cows like cows, and in each case they would make their bodies just in the form they themselves have. *Clement*

13 (B16)   Ethiopians say that their gods are snub-nosed and black, and Thracians that theirs have blue eyes and red hair. *Clement*

14 (B18)   Gods of course did not reveal everything to mortals from the beginning, but in time by searching they improve their discoveries. *Clement*

15 (B23)   One god, greatest among gods and men, not at all like mortals either in body or mind. *Clement*

16 (B24)   As a whole he sees, as a whole he thinks, and as a whole he hears. *Clement*

17 (B26)   And always he stays in the same place, not moving at all, nor is it fitting for him to travel in different directions at different times. *Simplicius*

18 (B25)   But with no effort at all he keeps everything moving by the thinking of his mind. *Simplicius*

19 (B29)   Everything that is born and growing is earth and water. *Simplicius*

20 (B27)   For all things are from earth and into earth all things come to their end. *Aetius*

21 (B33)   We all are generated from earth and water. *Sextus*

22 (B28)   The upper limit of earth is seen here at our feet, in contact with air; below it stretches on and on. *Achilles*

23 (B30)   The sea is the source of water and the source of wind; for without the great sea there would be <no wind> nor flowing rivers nor rain from the sky, but the great sea is the father of clouds and winds and rivers. *Aetius*

24 (B32)   And the one they call Iris – even this is by nature a cloud, purple and crimson and yellow to see. *Scholiast*

25 (B38)   If god had not made yellow honey, people would say that figs are much sweeter. *Herodian*

26 (B35)   Let these be accepted as opinions like the truth. *Plutarch*

27 (B34)   And so no man has seen anything clearly nor will there be anyone who knows about the gods and about what I say on everything; for if one should by chance speak about what has come to pass even as it is, still he himself does not *know*, but opinion is stretched over all. *Sextus*

28 (B7)   They say that once as he was passing by when a puppy was being beaten he took pity on it, and spoke as follows: "Stop! don't hit it! for it is the soul of a friend of mine, which I recognised when I heard its voice." *Diogenes*

Heraclitus of Ephesus

Logos, knowledge and perception

1 (B1)   Of the *logos*, which is as I describe it, people always prove to be uncomprehending both before they have heard it and once they have heard it. For, although all things happen according to the *logos*, people are like those of no experience, even when they do experience such words and deeds as I explain when I distinguish each thing according to its

phusis and declare how it is; but others fail to notice what they do after they wake up just as they forget what they do when asleep. *Sextus*

2 (B50)   Listening not to me but to the *logos* it is wise to agree that all is one. *Hippolytus*

3 (B89)   For those who are awake there is one common universe. *Plutarch*

4 (B41)   There is one wisdom, to understand how reason steers everything through everything. *Diogenes*

5 (B32)   The one and only wise does and does not consent to be called by the name of Zeus. *Clement*

6 (B113)   Thinking is common to all. *Stobaeus*

7 (B116)   All humans are able to know themselves and be prudent. *Stobaeus*

8 (B108)   Of all those whose *logoi* I have heard, no one reaches this conclusion – that the wise is separate from all things. *Stobaeus*

9 (B78)   Human nature [*ēthos*] has no wise thoughts [*gnōmai*], but the divine has. *Origen*

10 (B79)   A man is said to be a child compared with a god [*daimōn*], as is a child compared to a man. *Origen*

11 (B2)   One must follow what is common; but although the *logos* is common most people live as if they had a private understanding of their own. *Sextus*

12 (B34)   Not understanding after hearing they are like the deaf; they bear witness to the saying "absent when present." *Clement*

13 (B101a)   Eyes are more accurate witnesses than ears. *Polybius*

14 (B107)   Eyes and ears are bad witnesses for people who have souls that do not understand the language. *Sextus*

15 (B17)   Many who come across such things do not think about them, and even when they have learnt about them they do not understand, but to themselves they seem to. *Clement*

16 (B72)   Although people associate with *logos* most closely, they are separated from it, and what they come across every day seems to them strange. *Clement*

17 (B19)   They do not know how to listen or speak. *Clement*

18 (B73)   We must not speak and act like people asleep. *Clement*

19 (B95)   It is better to hide ignorance. *Plutarch*

20 (B35)   Men who love wisdom [*philosophoi*] must diligently research very many things. *Clement*

21 (B47)   Let's not make random guesses about the greatest matters. *Diogenes*

22 (B22)   Those who look for gold dig up much earth and find little. *Clement*

23 (B114)   Those who speak with sense must rely on what is common to all, as a city must rely on its law, and with much greater reliance; for all human laws are nourished by one divine law; for it has as much power as it wishes and is sufficient for all and is still not exhausted. *Stobaeus*

24 (B44)   The people must fight for the law as for their city wall. *Diogenes*

25 (B33)   It is law and custom to accept the ruling of one man. *Clement*

26 (B49)   One man is as ten thousand, if he is the best. *Galen*

27 (B39)   In Priene was born Bias, son of Teutamos, who had more *logos* than anyone else. *Diogenes*

28 (B18)   If you have no hope you will not find the unhoped-for, since it is undiscoverable and no path leads there. *Clements*

29 (B55)   All that is seen and heard and learnt I honour above all. *Hippolytus*

Strife, harmony and opposites

30 (B80)   You must know that war is common and justice is strife, and that all things happen by strife and necessity. *Origen*

31 (B53)   War is father of all and king of all: some he shows as gods, others as men; some he makes slaves, others free. *Hippolytus*

32 (B54)   Unseen *harmonia* is superior to that seen. *Hippolytus*

33 (B10)   Combinations: wholes and not wholes, being like and being different, in tune and out of tune, and from all things one, and from one all things. *Pseudo-Aristotle*

34 (B8)   Opposites come together and from what is different arises the fairest *harmonia*. *Aristotle*

35 (B9)   Donkeys would choose rubbish rather than gold. *Aristotle*

36 (B13)   Pigs enjoy mud rather than clean water. *Clement*

37 (B61)   Sea water is most pure and most polluted; for fish it is drinkable, but for humans undrinkable and destructive. *Hippolytus*

38 (B11)   Every animal is driven to pasture with a blow. *Pseudo-Aristotle*

39 (B59)   The path of letters is straight and crooked. *Hippolytus*

40 (B60)   Way up, way down: one and the same. *Hippolytus*

41 (B48)   For the bow the name means life, but its work is death. *Etymologion*

42 (B111)   Disease makes health pleasant and good, as does hunger satiety and weariness rest. *Sextus*

43 (B7)   If all that there is turned to smoke, the nose would distinguish between them. *Aristotle*

44 (B97)   Dogs bark at those they do not recognise. *Plutarch*

45 (B126)   Cold things warm, warm cools, wet dries, parched is moistened. *Tzetzes*

46 (B96)   Corpses are more disposable than dung. *Plutarch*

47 (B102)   To god all things are beautiful and good and just, but humans have supposed some to be unjust, others just. *Porphyry*

48 (B67)   God: day night; winter summer; war peace; satiety hunger; but he changes like <fire>, which, when mingled with the smoke of incense, is named according to each individual's perception. *Hippolytus*

49 (B51)   They do not understand that what conflicts with itself agrees with itself: there is a *harmonia* of opposite tensions, as in the bow and lyre. *Hippolytus*

50 (B125)   The barley-drink separates if it is not stirred. *Theophrastus*

51 (B84a)   Changing it rests. *Plotinus*

52 (B123)   Nature likes to hide. *Themistius*

53 (B23)   They would not know the name of *Dikē* if these <opposites> did not exist. *Clement*

54 (B52)   Time is a child playing draughts; the kingship is a child's. *Hippolytus*

Fire, flux and cosmology

55 (B91)   It is not possible to step twice into the same river. *Plutarch*

56 (B12)   Over those who step into the same rivers ever different waters flow. *Arius*

57 (B30)   This order, the same for all, no one of gods or men has made, but it always was and is and will be, ever-living fire, kindled in measures and extinguished in measures. *Clement*

58 (B64)   Thunderbolt steers all things. *Hippolytus*

59 (B66)   Fire, having caught up with them, will judge and constrain all things. *Hippolytus*

60 (B94)   Sun will not overstep his measures, otherwise the Erinyes, ministers of justice, will find him out. *Plutarch*

61 (B3)   <sun> breadth of a man's foot *Aetius*

62 (B6)   The sun is new every day. *Aristotle*

63 (B99)   If there were no sun, as far as depended on the other stars it would be night. *Plutarch*

64 (B100)   <the sun> governs the hours/seasons which bring all things. *Plutarch*

65 (B16)   How could one hide from that which never sets? *Clement*

66 (B120)   The limits of morning and evening are the Bear, and opposite the Bear is the boundary of Zeus of the sky above. *Strabo*

67 (B90)   All things are an equal exchange for fire and fire for all things, as goods are for gold and gold for goods. *Plutarch*

68 (B31)   The changes of fire: first sea, and of sea half earth and half lightning flash; earth is poured out as sea and is measured in the same proportion as it was before it became earth. *Clement*

69 (B124)   The cosmos, most beautiful, is as a rubbish heap piled up at random. *Theophrastus*

Psychology and ethics, life and death

70 (B45)   You could not in your going find the limits of soul though you travelled the whole way – so deep is its *logos*. *Diogenes*

71 (B101)   I searched myself. *Plutarch*

72 (B115)   There is *logos* of soul which increases itself. *Stobaeus*

73 (B118)   Dry soul is wisest and best. *Stobaeus*

74 (B119)   A person's character is his destiny. *Stobaeus*

75 (B112)   The greatest virtue is to be prudent, and wisdom is to speak the truth and to act with understanding according to nature. *Stobaeus*

76 (B110)   It is not better for people to get what they want. *Sextus*

77 (B98)   Souls have the sense of smell in Hades. *Plutarch*

78 (B36)   For souls it is death to become water, for water death to become earth; from earth arises water, and from water soul. *Clement*

79 (B77)   It is delight or death for souls to become wet [...] we live their death and they live our death. *Numenius*

80 (B84b)   It is weariness for the same people to labour and to be subject to commands. *Plotinus*

81 (B85)   It is hard to fight against impulse; whatever it wants it buys at the expense of soul. *Plutarch*

82 (B117)   When a man is drunk he is led stumbling along by a boy, having his soul wet. *Stobaeus*

83 (B24)   Gods and men honour the war-dead. *Clement*

84 (B29)   The best choose one thing above all: everlasting fame among men; but most gorge themselves like cattle. *Clement*

85 (B25)   Greater fates are allotted greater destinies. *Clement*

86 (B27)   When men have died there awaits them what they neither expected nor imagined. *Clement*

87 (B63)   When the god is there they rise up and become watchful guardians of the living and the dead. *Hippolytus*

88 (B20)   Having come to birth they want to live and have their fates, and they leave children behind to become their fates. *Clement*

89 (B21)   Death is what we see when awake, and what we see asleep is sleep. *Clement*

90 (B88)   As the same thing there exist in us living and dead, waking and sleeping, young and old; for these change round and are those, and those change round and are these. *Plutarch*

91 (B26)   A man in the night kindles/touches a light for himself because his seeing has been put out; when alive, while he sleeps, he touches the dead, and, while he is awake, he touches the sleeping. *Clement*

92 (B75)   People asleep are workers, taking part in the work of the cosmos. *Marcus Antoninus*

93 (B62)   Immortals are mortal, mortals immortal, living the death of those, and dying the life of these. *Hippolytus*

94 (B88)   It is the same in <us>: being alive and dead, awake and asleep and young and old; for these, after changing, are those, and those again, after changing, are these. *Plutarch*

Counterfeit learning and religion

95 (B40)   Much learning does not teach anyone to get understanding; otherwise it would have taught Hesiod and Pythagoras, and also Xenophanes and Hecataeus. *Diogenes*

96 (B57)   Hesiod is the teacher of very many, whom they know understands very much; but he did not recognise day and night, for they are one. *Hippolytus*

97 (B42)   Homer deserves to be thrown out of the contests and given a beating, and Archilochus as well. *Diogenes*

98 (B56)   Humans are tricked in the understanding of what is obvious, just like Homer, who was wiser than all the Greeks. For children who were killing lice tricked him saying: "what we saw and seized we left behind, but what we did not see or seize, this we took with us." *Hippolytus*

99 (B43)   Pride should be quenched more than a fire. *Diogenes*

100 (B5)   When polluted they purify themselves by washing with another's blood, as if you could clean off mud by stepping into mud. But a man would be thought mad if anyone were to see him behaving in this way. And they pray to their statues like someone talking to a house, not knowing the nature of gods and heroes. *Origen*

101 (B14)   Night-prowlers, magicians, bacchants, maenads, mystics; the rites men practise in the holy mysteries are unholy. *Clement*

102 (B58)   Doctors do nothing that deserves taking payment when they cut and burn, doing the same in the cure as the illness. *Hippolytus*

103 (B15)   If it were not in honour of Dionysus that they walk in procession and sing a hymn to the phallus they would be acting most shamelessly. Hades and Dionysus, for whom they rave in frenzy, are the same. *Clement*

104 (B92)   The Sibyl with raving mouth utters sounds from the god without humour or elegance or fragrance. *Plutarch*

105 (B93)   The lord whose oracle is at Delphi neither speaks nor conceals but gives a sign. *Plutarch*

106 (B28)   The one who appears most wise knows only appearances and stays by them. But justice will catch up with the architects of lies and perjurers. *Clement*

107 (B87)   A foolish person gets excited at every *logos*. *Plutarch*

Parmenides of Elea

The proem

1 (B1)   The mares, which carry me as far as my heart desires, were driving me, when they took me up as they travelled along to the famous road of the goddess, which leads a man of learning through all the towns. There I was driven, for the clever horses pulled me along, straining at the carriage, and girls were guiding them on their way. The axle in the naves let out the shrill sound of a pipe as the sparks flew (for the two wheels on either side were whirring round), while the girls, the daughters of the Sun, sped on, leaving the realm of Night for the light, tossing back the veils from their heads with their hands (1–10). The gates of the roads of Night and Day are there, bounded by a lintel above and a stone threshold. They contain great doors that rise high in the air, and avenging Justice keeps the keys which fit them. The girls, flattering her with

soft words, skillfully persuaded her to pull back without delay the bar that bolted the gates; and the doors, swinging on their hinges the two bronze panels fitted with bolts and rivets, were flung apart, and revealed a yawning opening. Straight through, along a broad highway, the girls drove the chariot and horses (11–21). Then a goddess graciously received me. She took my right hand in hers, and addressed me with these words: Young man, coming to our home in the company of immortal chariot-eers, with their horses driving you, welcome! It is no ill chance which has sent you to travel along this road, far from the way trodden by humans, but right and justice. You must learn about everything, both the unshaken heart of well-rounded truth and the opinions of mortals, in which there is no true belief; nevertheless you shall learn about these too – that what seems to exist really does, all inclusively (22–32). *Sextus*

2 (B2)   Come now, pay heed to my account and take it with you – I shall tell you only the ways of enquiry that are to be thought of: that it is and cannot not be is the path of persuasion, for it attends on truth, that it is not, and necessarily is not, is, I tell you, a path of which nothing can be learnt, for you could not recognise what is not (that is impossible) nor name it [...]. *Proclus*

3 (B3)   [F]or what can be thought of is the same as what can be. *Clement*

4 (B4)   Contemplate steadily what is absent as present to your mind; for it will never cut off what is from holding to what it is, since it neither scatters in every direction in every away nor draws together in order. *Clement*

5 (B5)   It does not matter to me where I begin; for I shall return there again. *Proclus*

6 (B6)   What can be spoken and thought of must exist, for it *can* exist but nothing can not; this I bid you ponder. This is the first way of enquiry from which I hold you back, and then from this second one too, along which men wander – knowing nothing, two headed, for helpless-ness steers the wandering thought in their hearts. They move along deaf as well as blind, dazed uncritical crowds, who consider to be and not to be the same and not the same, and that for all things there is a path turning back again. *Simplicius*

7 (B7)   It shall never be proved that what-is-not is; keep your thought from this way of enquiry, and do not let habit-forming custom cause your heedless eye and echoing ear and your tongue to mislead you, but judge by reasoning the hard-hitting argument reported by me. *Simplicius*

The Way of Truth (Alētheia)

8 (B8)   One way only is left to speak of, namely that it is. Along this way are many signs: that what-is is *ungenerated* and *indestructible, unique, unmoved* and *complete*; it never was nor will be, since it is now all together *one and continuous* (1–6). What creation will you seek for it? how did it grow? and from what source? I will not allow you to say or to think 'from what is not,' for it is not possible to say or to think what is not. And if it did come from nothing what compulsion was there for it to arise later rather than earlier? therefore it must either be all at once or not at all. And the strength of conviction will not allow anything else ever to arise from what is not. That is why Justice does not relax her bonds and allow what is to come to be or pass away, but holds it fast. The decision on this rests here: it is or it is not – that is why it is decided, as it must be, to dismiss the one as not to be thought or named (for it is not the way of truth) and to take the other as really existing. How could what-is later perish? how could it come into existence? for if it came into existence in the past or if it is going to exist at some time in the future it is not; so generation is extinguished and destruction incredible (7–21). It is not divisible, since it is all alike; nor is there more [of it] at one time and less at another which would prevent its continuity, but all is full of what there is. So that it all holds together, for what-is stays close to what-is (22–25). Moreover, without beginning and without end (since generation and destruction have been driven afar, and true conviction has cast them out) it is immobile in the bonds of great chains. Remaining the same and in the same it abides by itself and so stays firm, for harsh necessity keeps it in the chains of the limit which holds it around, because it is not right for what-is to be incomplete; for it is not in need – if it were it would need everything (26–35). What is there to be thought of is the same as what is thought, for you will not find thinking apart from what-is, which is what is referred to. There is and will be nothing apart from what-is, since Fate holds this as one and unchanged. But this has been given all the names that people have proposed, in their conviction of the truth – birth and death, being and not being, shift of place and change of bright colour (34–41). Moreover, since it is utterly unchanging, it is complete on every side, like the bulk of a well-rounded sphere, equally balanced about the centre in every direction, for it cannot be more here and less there than what-is, since it is all continuous; being equal to itself on every side it rests uniformly in its limits (42–49).

The Way of Opinion (Doxa)

[8 (B8), cont.]   Here I end my reliable argument and thought concerning truth. From this point on learn about the opinions of humans, as you listen to the deceptive arrangement of my words. People have made up their minds to name two forms; they should not name even one of them – that is where they have gone astray. They have distinguished them as opposites in appearance, and assigned them marks distinct from one another – to one the aetherial flame of fire, gentle and very fine, identical with itself in every direction but different from the other. The other is its opposite – dark night, a heavy and composite body. I am telling you the whole plausible arrangement of them, so that no one's thinking shall outpace you (50–61). *Simplicius*

9 (B9)   Since all things have been named light and night, and the names which belong to the powers of each have been assigned, all is full at once of light and dark night, both equal, since nothing is without either. *Simplicius*

10 (B10)   You shall know the nature of the sky and all the signs in the sky, and the unseen functioning of the shining sun's clear torch and how it arose, and you will learn of the wandering actions of the round-faced moon and its nature, and you will understand how the surrounding heaven came about and how necessity brought it to hold fast the limits of the stars. *Clement*

11 (B11)   [...] how earth and sun and moon and universal sky [*aethēr*] and the <galaxy of the> Milky Way and the hot force of the stars rushed into being. *Simplicius*

12 (B13)   first of all the gods was Eros devised. *Plato*

13 (B14)   A borrowed light shining in the night wanders round earth. *Plutarch*

14 (B15)   always looking to the rays of the sun *Plutarch*

15 (B12)   For the narrower <circles> were filled with unmixed fire, and those next to them with night, but alongside an allotted amount of fire; and in the middle of these the goddess who governs all. For she controls everything belonging to harsh birth and intercourse, sending the female to unite with the male and again, the other way round, the male to the female. *Simplicius*

16 (B17)   on the right boys and on the left girls *Galen*

17 (B16)   According to the nature of the mixture of the wandering limbs that each one has, so does thought stand for each; that which

thinks, the nature of the limbs, is the same for each and everyone; and what there is more of *is* that thought. *Aristotle*

18 (B19)   According to belief they were and are now, and, in the future, after their maturity, they will come to an end; and people have given each of them a distinctive name. *Simplicius*

Zeno of Elea

Zeno's support of Parmenides: If there are many things then:

How many are they (1)?
How big are they (2), (3)?
Do they make a noise (6)?
Where are they (5)?
How can they move (4), (6)?

1 (B3)   If there are many things, (i) they will be just as many as they are, no more and no less; and if they are just as many as they are, they would be limited (in number).

If there are many things, (ii) the things that there are are unlimited; for there will always be other things between the things that there are, and again other things between them, and so the things that there are are unlimited (in number). *Simplicius*

2 (B1)   If what exists has no size, it would not exist. But if it does exist each thing must have some size and thickness, and one part of it must be distinct from another. And there is the same argument for what is in front, for that will have size and some part of it will be in front. Indeed, to say this once is similar to saying it for ever, for no such part of it will be the last or the same as a further part. Therefore, if there are many things, they must be both small and great: so small as to have no size, and so big as to be unlimited (in size). *Simplicius*

3 (B2)   If it were added to something else, it would not make it any bigger; for if it has no size at all and were added on, it would not contribute any increase in size, and so what is now being added on would be nothing. And if, while it is being subtracted, the other will be no smaller it is obvious that what was added or subtracted was nothing. *Simplicius*

4 (B4)   What moves does not move in the place in which it is *or* in the place in which it is not. *Diogenes*

5 (A24)   If there is a place for the things that are, where would it be? It would be in another place and *that* in another place and so on. *Eudemus*

6 (A29)

ZENO:	Tell me Protagoras, does a single millet seed make a noise as it falls, or does 1/10,000 of a millet?
PROTAGORAS:	No.
ZENO:	Does a bushel of millet seed make a noise as it falls, or not?
PROTAGORAS:	Yes, a bushel makes a noise.
ZENO:	But isn't there a ratio (*logos*) between a bushel of millet seed, and one seed, and 1/10,000 of a seed?
PROTAGORAS:	Yes, there is.
ZENO:	So won't there be the same ratio of sounds between them, for the sounds are in proportion to what makes the sound? And, if this is so, if the bushel of millet seed makes a noise so will a single seed and 1/10,000 of a seed. *Simplicius*

7 (A25–28)   Zeno has four propositions [*logoi*] about movement which are puzzling for those who try to solve them:

   i   The Dichotomy: it is impossible to move from one place to another

The first argument about there being no movement says that the moving object must first reach the halfway mark before the end – and the quarter-mark before the half, and so back, so there is no first move; and the three-quarter mark after the half, and so forward, so that there is no last move.

   ii   The Achilles: Achilles cannot overtake the tortoise

The second is the one called Achilles. This is it: the slowest will never be overtaken in running by the fastest, for the pursuer must always come to the point the pursued has left, so that the slower must always be some (proportionate) distance ahead.

   iii   The Arrow: the moving arrow is at rest

The third one mentioned is that the moving arrow is at rest. The arrow is at rest at any time when it occupies a space just its own length, and yet it is always moving at any time in its flight (i.e. in the 'now'), therefore the moving arrow is motionless.

   iv   The Stadium: a time is twice itself

The fourth is the one about equal blocks moving past equal blocks from opposite directions in the stadium – one set from the end of the stadium and one from the middle – at the same speed; here he thinks that half the time is equal to twice itself. For example: AAAA are equal stationary blocks, BBBB, equal to them in number and size, are beginning from the half-way point (of the stadium), CCCC equal to these also in size, and equal to the Bs in speed, are coming towards them from the end. It happens of course that the first B reaches the end at the same time as the first C as they move past each other. And it happens that the C passes all the Bs but the Bs only half (the As) so the time is then half itself. *Aristotle*

Melissus of Samos

1 (B1) What was always was, and always shall be, for, if it came into being, before its generation there would have to be nothing; therefore, if there were nothing, nothing at all would come from nothing. *Simplicius*

2 (B2) Since then it did not come into being, it is and always was and always shall be, and has neither beginning nor end, but is without limit. For if it had come into being, it would have a beginning (for it would have begun to come into being at some time) and an end (for it would have stopped coming into being at some time); but, since it neither began nor ended, it always was and shall be and has no beginning nor end; for it is impossible for the incomplete to be everlasting. *Simplicius*

3 (B3) But as it always is, so too it is without limit in extent. *Simplicius*

4 (B4) No thing that has both beginning and end is eternal or without limit. *Simplicius*

5 (B5) If it were not one thing, it would limit some other thing. *Simplicius*

6 (B6) For if it were without limit, it would be one; for if there were two, they could not be without limit, one would limit the other. *Simplicius*

7 (B7)

i So therefore it is eternal and without limit, one and a homogenous whole.

ii And it cannot pass away or become greater or change its arrangement or feel pain or be distressed; for if it could suffer any of these it would not still be one. For if it were to change, what there is could not be homogenous, but what is in front would pass away, and what does not exist would come into existence. If therefore it were to become different by as much as a single hair in ten thousand years, it would all pass away in the whole of time.

iii   It is impossible for there to be a change in arrangement; for the *kosmos* which was before does not pass away, nor does one which is not come into existence. And since nothing at all is added or passes away or is altered how can there be a change in the existing *kosmos?* for if it became different in any way, immediately there would be a change in the *kosmos*.

iv   And it does not feel pain; for anything in pain could not exist for ever, and it does not have as much power as what is healthy. And if it were in pain it would not be homogenous, for it would feel pain from the loss or addition of something, and would no longer be homogenous.

v   The healthy could not feel pain, for then the healthy, what there is, would pass away, and what is not would come to be.

vi   The same argument applies to distress as to pain.

vii   It is not empty at all; for what is empty is nothing, and then what is nothing could not be. And it does not move; for it cannot retreat in any direction, but it is full. For if it were empty it would retreat into the empty; but since the empty does not exist, it has nowhere to retreat to.

viii   And it would not be dense and rare; for it is not possible for what is rare to be full in the same way as what is dense, but the rare of course is emptier than the dense.

ix   This distinction must be made between what is full and what is not full: if it retreats or takes in anything it is not full, but if it does not retreat or take in anything it is full.

x   So it must be full, since there is no empty. If then it is full, it does not move. *Simplicius*

8 (B8)   This argument then provides the strongest proof that it is one only; but there are these proofs as well:

i   If there were many things they would have to be such as I say the one is. For if there is earth and water and air and fire and iron and gold, and one living and another dead, and again black and white and all the other things that people say are true and real, if indeed these things exist and we see and hear them correctly, each must be such as we first decided, and they cannot change or become different, but each is always as it is.

ii   But we do say that we see and hear and perceive correctly, and yet it seems to us that the hot becomes cold and the cold hot, and the hard becomes soft and the soft hard, and the living dies and there is birth from what is not living, and all these things change around. What a thing was and what it is now are not at all the same, but iron, which is hard, is rubbed away by contact with the finger, and also gold and stone and whatever seems to us to be strong, and from water come earth and stone, so it happens that we do not see or understand what there really is.

iii   These claims do not agree with each other. We say that many things are constant, and have forms and strength, but they all seem to us to become different from what we see at any given moment. It is clear therefore that we were not seeing correctly, and that those many things do not appear as they rightly are, for they would not change if they were real, but each would be as it seemed, for nothing is stronger than what really exists.

iv   If it were to change, what is is destroyed and what is not has come to be; therefore, if there were many things, they would each have to be as the one is. *Simplicius*

9 (B9)   So if it exists it must be one; and being one it could not have body. If it had thickness it would have parts, and would no longer be one. *Simplicius*

10 (B10)   If what exists is divided, it moves: and if it moves it would not exist. *Simplicius*

Empedocles of Acragas

On Nature

1 (B2)   The powers spread over the body are constricted, and many afflictions burst in and dull their meditations. After observing a small part of their life in their lifetime, subject to a swift death they are borne up and waft away like smoke; they are convinced only of that which each has experienced as they are driven in all directions, yet all boast of finding the whole. These things are not so to be seen or heard by men or grasped with mind. But you now, since you have come aside to this place, will learn within the reach of human understanding. *Sextus*

2 (B3)   But turn from my tongue, o gods, the madness of these men, and from hallowed lips let a pure stream flow. And I entreat you, virgin

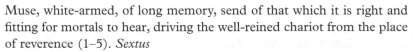

Muse, white-armed, of long memory, send of that which it is right and fitting for mortals to hear, driving the well-reined chariot from the place of reverence (1–5). *Sextus*

3 (B131)   If for the sake of any one of mortals, immortal Muse, our cares came to your attention, now once more, Kalliopeia, answer a prayer, and support the unfolding of a worthy account of the blessed gods. *Hippolytus*

4 (B1)   Heed my words, Pausanias, son of wise Anchitos. *Diogenes*

5 (B3)   But do not let them impel you to take up garlands of glory and honour from mortals, on condition that you speak recklessly, over-stepping propriety, and so then sit on the high throne of wisdom. But come, observe with every power in what way each thing is clear, without considering any seeing more reliable compared with hearing, nor echoing ear above piercings of the tongue; and do not keep back trust at all from the other parts of the body by which there is a channel for understand-ing, but understand each particular in the way in which it is clear (6–13). *Sextus*

6 (B4)   It is indeed the habit of the mischievous to distrust authority, but learn yourself as the assurances of my Muse urge, once the argument has been articulated within your breast. *Clement*

7 (B6)   Hear first the four roots of all things: bright Zeus and life-bringing Hera and Aidoneus and Nestis, whose tears are the source of mortal streams. *Aetius*

8 (B17)   A twofold tale I shall tell: at one time it grew to be only one from many, and at another again it divided to be many from one. There is a double birth of what is mortal, and a double passing away: for the uniting of all things brings one generation into being and destroys it, and the other is reared and scattered as they are again being divided. And these things never cease their continual exchange of position, at one time all coming together into one through love, at another again being borne away from each other by strife's repulsion. <So, in so far as one is accustomed to arise from many> and many are produced from one as it is again being divided, to this extent they are born and have no abiding life; but in so far as they never cease their continual exchange, so far they are forever unaltered in the cycle (1–13). But come, hear my words, for learning brings an increase of wisdom. Even as I said before, when I was stating the range of my discourse, a twofold tale I shall tell: at one time it grew to be only one from many, and at another again it divided to be many from one – fire and water and earth and measureless height of air, with pernicious strife apart from these, matched <to them> in

every direction, and love among them, their equal in length and breadth. Contemplate her with the mind, and do not sit staring dazed; she is acknowledged to be inborn also in the bodies of men, and because of her their thoughts are friendly and they work together, giving her the name Joy, as well as Aphrodite. No mortal has perceived her as she whirls among them; but you now attend to the progress of my argument, which does not mislead (14–26). All these are equal and of like age, but each has a different prerogative and its own particular character, and they prevail in turn as the time comes round. Furthermore, nothing comes to birth later in addition to these, and there is no passing away, for if they were continually perishing they would no longer exist. And what would increase this whole, and from where would it come? How would it be completely destroyed, since nothing is without them? No, these are the only real things, but as they run through each other they become different objects at different times, yet they are forever the same (27–35). *Simplicius*

9 (B12)   It is impossible for there to be coming into existence from what is not, and for what exists to be completely destroyed cannot be achieved, and is unheard of; for where it is thrust at any time, there it will always be. *Pseudo-Aristotle*

10 (B13)   There is no part of the whole that is empty or overfull. *Aetius*

11 (B16)   They are as they were before, and so shall be, and never, I think, will endless time be emptied of these two. *Hippolytus*

12 (B8)   Here is another point: of all mortal things none has birth or any end in pernicious death, but there is only a mixing and a separating of what has been mixed, and to these people give the name 'birth.' *Plutarch*

13 (B9)   When they have been mixed in the form of a man and come to the air, or in the form of the race of wild animals, or of plants, or of birds, then people say that this is 'to be born,' and, when they separate, they call this again 'ill-fated death'; these terms are not right, but I follow the custom and use them myself. *Plutarch*

14 (B21)   But come, if the form of my preceding argument was in any way incomplete, take note of the witnesses of these to what I have said before: sun with its radiant appearance and pervading warmth, heavenly bodies bathed in heat and shining light, rain everywhere dark and chill, and from earth issue firmly-rooted solids. Under strife they have different forms and are all separate, but they come together in love and are desired by one another. From them comes all that was and is

and will be hereafter – trees have sprung from them, and men and women, and animals and birds and water-nourished fish, and long-lived gods too, highest in honour. For these are the only real things, and, as they run through each other, they assume different forms, as the mixing interchanges them. *Simplicius*

15 (B23)   As painters, men well taught by wisdom in the practice of their art, decorate temple offerings – they take in their hands pigments of various colours, and after fitting them in close combination, more of some and less of others, they produce from them shapes resembling all things, creating trees and men and women, animals and birds and water-nourished fish, and long-lived gods too, highest in honour; so do not let your mind be deceived into thinking that there is any other source for the countless perishables that are seen, but know this clearly, since the discourse you have heard is from a god. *Simplicius*

16 (B26)   They prevail in turn as the cycle moves round, and decrease into each other and increase in appointed succession. For these are the only real things, and, as they run through one another, they become men and the kinds of other animals – at one time coming into one order through love, at another again being borne away from each other by strife's hate, until they come together into the whole and are subdued. So, in so far as one is accustomed to arise from many, and many are produced from one as it is again being divided, to this extent they are born and have no abiding life; but in so far as they never cease their continual exchange, they are for ever unaltered in the cycle. *Simplicius*

17 (B25)   For what is right is worth repeating. *Plato*

18 (B24)   Joining one main point to another, so as not to pursue only one path of discourse [...]. *Plutarch*

19 (B36)   Strife was retreating from them to the extremity as they were coming together. *Stobaeus*

20 (B27a)   No anarchy or unseemly fighting in the parts [...]. *Plutarch*

21 (B27)   There the swift limbs of the sun are not distinguished, nor the shaggy might of earth, nor sea; in this way it is held fast in the close covering of harmony, a rounded sphere, rejoicing in encircling stillness. *Simplicius*

22 (B29, 28)   For two branches do not spring from his back, he has no feet, no swift knees, no genitals, but he is equal to himself in every direction, a rounded sphere, rejoicing in encircling stillness. *Hippolytus, Stobaeus*

23 (B30)   But when strife had grown great in the frame and leapt upward to its honours as the time was being completed, which is fixed for them in turn by a broad oath [...]. *Simplicius*

24 (B31)   One by one all the parts of the god began to tremble. *Simplicius*

25 (B22)   For all these – sun and earth and sky and sea – are one with the parts of themselves that have been separated from them and born in mortal things. In the same way, those that are more ready to combine are made similar by Aphrodite and feel mutual affection. But such as are most different from each other in birth and mixture and in the moulding of their forms are most hostile, with no experience of union, and grieving deeply at their generation in strife, in that they were born in anger. *Simplicius*

26 (B20)   This is well known in the mass of mortal limbs: at one time, in the maturity of a vigorous life, all the limbs that are the body's portion come into one under love; at another time again, torn asunder by evil quarrels, they wander, each apart, on the shore of life, So it is too for plants, and for fish that live in the water, and for wild animals who have their lairs in the hills, and for the wing-sped gulls. *Simplicius*

27 (B38)   Come now, I shall tell you from what sources in the beginning <came> the sun and all the others which we now see become distinct – earth and swelling sea and moist air and Titan sky, whose circle binds fast all things. *Clement*

28 (B51)   [...] swiftly upwards [...]. *Herodian*

29 (B53)   For it chanced to be running in this way then, but often in other ways. *Aristotle*

30 (B54)   Air with deep roots sank down over the earth. *Aristotle*

31 (B37)   Earth increases its own bulk, and air increases air. *Aristotle*

32 (B52)   Many fires burn beneath the surface of the earth. *Proclus*

33 (B39)   If the depths of the earth and extensive air are without limit, as has come foolishly from the tongue of the mouths of many who have seen but a little of the whole [...]. *Aristotle*

34 (B40)   [...] sharp-arrowed sun and kindly moon [...]. *Plutarch*

35 (B41)   But <the sun>, after being collected together, moves round the great sky. *Apollodorus*

36 (B44)   He shines back to Olympus with fearless face. *Plutarch*

37 (B47)   She contemplates the bright circle of her lord facing her. *Anecdota Graeca*

38 (B43)   As the ray, after striking the broad circle of the moon [...]. *Plutarch*

39 (B45)   A circle of borrowed light moves swiftly round the earth. *Achilles*

40 (B46)   As the course of the chariot turns round and back, she [...]. *Plutarch*

41 (B42)   She dispersed his rays to earth from the upper side, and cast on the earth a shadow equal to the breadth of the silvery moon. *Plutarch*

42 (B48)   And earth causes night by coming under the rays. *Plutarch*

43 (B49)   [...] of desolate, blind-eyed night [...]. *Plutarch*

44 (B50)   Iris brings wind or heavy rain from the sea. *Tzetzes*

45 (B56)   Salt was crystallised under pressure from the rays of the sun. *Hephaestus*

46 (B55)   [...] sea, sweat of earth [...]. *Aristotle*

47 (B35)   But I shall turn back to the path of song I traced before, leading off from one explanation [*logos*] this one: when strife had reached the lowest depth of the whirl and love comes into the centre of the eddy, in her then all these things unite to be one only – not immediately, but coming together from different directions at will. And, as they were being mixed, countless types of mortal things poured forth, although many, which strife still restrained from above, stayed unmixed, alternating with those that were combining, for it had not yet perfectly and completely stood out as far as the furthest limits of the circle, but part remained within and part had gone out of the frame. And, in proportion as it continually ran on ahead, a mild, immortal onrush of perfect love was continually pursuing it. Immediately what were formerly accustomed to be immortal became mortal, and formerly unmixed things were in a mixed state, owing to the exchanging of their ways. And, as they are being mixed, countless types of mortal things pour forth, fitted with all kinds of forms, a wonder to see. *Simplicius*

48 (B96)   And the kindly earth received into its broad hollows of the eight parts two of the brightness of Nestis and four of Hephaistos; and these came to be white bones, marvelously held together by the gluing of harmony. *Simplicius*

49 (B34)   When he had glued barley meal with water [...]. *Aristotle*

50 (B57)   Here many heads sprang up without necks, bare arms were wandering without shoulders, and eyes needing foreheads strayed on their own. *Simplicius*

51 (B59)   But as god mingled further with god they fell together as they chanced to meet each other, and many other things in addition to these were continually arising. *Simplicius*

52 (B61)   Many creatures with a face and breasts on both sides were produced, man-faced bulls and again bull-headed men, <others> with male and female nature combined, and the bodies they had were dark. *Aelian, Simplicius*

53 (B62)   And now hear this – how fire, as it was being separated, brought up by night the shoots of men and pitiable women, for the account is to the point and well informed. First whole-nature forms, having a share of both water and heat, sprang up from the earth; fire, as it tended to reach its like, kept sending them up, when they did not yet show the lovely shape of the limbs, or voice or language native to men. *Simplicius*

54 (B65)   They were poured in pure places; some met with cold and became women [...]. *Aristotle*

55 (B67)   For the male was in the warmer part [...] this is the reason why men are dark, more powerfully built and hairier. *Galen*

56 (B68)   On the tenth day of the eighth month it became a white pus. *Aristotle*

57 (B71)   But if your belief about these things in any way lacked assurance, how, from the combining of water, earth, air and sun came the forms and colour of mortal things which have now arisen, fitted together by Aphrodite [...]. *Simplicius*

58 (B73)   At that time, when Cypris was busily producing forms, she moistened earth in water and gave it to swift fire to harden. *Simplicius*

59 (B72)   How tall trees and fishes in the sea [...]. *Athenaeus*

60 (B77/8)   Trees ever-bearing leaves and ever-bearing fruit flourish with an abundance of fruit because of the air all the year round. *Theophrastus*

61 (B79)   In this way tall trees produce olive eggs first. *Aristotle*

62 (B80)   This is why pomegranates come late in the season, and apples are exceptionally succulent. *Plutarch*

63 (B81)   Water from the bark, fermented in wood, becomes wine. *Plutarch*

64 (B76)   This <happens> with the hard-backed shells of those who live in the sea, especially in sea-snails and stony-skinned turtles; there you will notice that earth stays on the top surface. *Plutarch*

65 (B75/99)   Of those which are compact within and loosely formed on the outside, having met with this kind of flaccidity at the hand of Cypris [...] <ear> a fleshy growth [...]. *Simplicius, Theophrastus*

66 (B82)   As the same things grow hair, leaves, the close-packed feathers of birds, and scales on strong limbs. *Aristotle*

67 (B83)   but for hedgehogs sharp-pointed hairs bristle on their backs [...]. *Plutarch*

68 (B89)   There are effluences from all things in existence. *Plutarch*

69 (B91)   <Water> combines more with wine, but refuses with oil. *Alexander*

70 (B90)   So sweet seized on sweet, bitter rushed to bitter, sour came to sour and hot coupled with hot. *Plutarch*

71 (B93)   And the gleam of bright saffron mixes in with the linen. *Plutarch*

72 (B109)   With earth we perceive earth, with water water, with air divine air, with fire destructive fire, with love love, and strife with baneful strife. *Aristotle*

73 (B107)   All things are fitted together and constructed out of these, and by means of them they think and feel pleasure and pain. *Theophrastus*

74 (B106)   People's wisdom grows according to what is present. *Aristotle*

75 (B108)   In so far as they have changed in their nature, so far changed thoughts are always present to them. *Aristotle*

76 (B103)   There by the working of chance all things have conscious thoughts. *Simplicius*

77 (B98)   And earth, anchored in the perfect harbours of Aphrodite, chanced to come together with them in almost equal quantities, with Hephaistos and rain and all-shining air, either a little more, or less where there was more. From these came blood and forms of other flesh. *Simplicius*

78 (B85)   The gentle flame met with a slight portion of earth. *Simplicius*

79 (B86)   Out of these the goddess Aphrodite fashioned untiring eyes. *Simplicius*

80 (B95)   When they first grew together in the hands of Cypris [...]. *Simplicius*

81 (B84)   As when a man who intends to make a journey prepares a light for himself, a flame of fire burning through a wintry night; he fits linen screens against all the winds which break the blast of the winds as they blow, but the light that is more diffuse leaps through, and shines across the threshold with unfailing beams. In the same way the elemental fire, wrapped in membranes and delicate tissues, was then concealed in the round pupil – these kept back the surrounding deep water, but let through the more diffuse light. *Aristotle*

82 (B88)   From both <eyes> comes one seeing. *Aristotle*

83 (B100)   This is the way in which all things breathe in and out. They all have channels of flesh, which the blood leaves, stretched over the surface of the body, and at the mouth of these the outside of the skin is pierced right through with close-set holes, so that blood is contained, but a passage is cut for air to pass through freely. Then, when the smooth blood rushes away from the surface, a wild surge of blustering air rushes through, and, when the blood leaps up, the air breathes out again. It is like a girl playing with a clepsydra of shining bronze – when she puts the mouth of the pipe against her pretty hand and dips it into the smooth body of shining water, no liquid yet enters the vessel, but the mass of air pressing from within against the close-set perforations holds it back until she releases the compressed current, and then, as air escapes, a due amount of water enters (1–15). Similarly, when she has water in the hollow of the bronze vessel, and the neck and passage are closed by human hand, the air outside, pressing inward, keeps the water in at the gates of the harsh-sounding strainer, controlling the defences, until the girl releases her hand; then, the reverse of the former process – as the air rushes in, a due amount of water runs out before it. In the same way, when the smooth blood surging through the body rushes back and inward, a flooding stream of air at once comes pouring in, and, when the blood leaps up, an equal amount <of air> in turn breathes back out again (16–25). *Aristotle*

84 (B101)   [T]racking with nostrils fragments of animal bodies <which they> left behind from their feet on the smooth grass. *Plutarch, Alexander*

85 (B102)   In this way all things are apportioned breathing and smelling. *Theophrastus*

86 (B105)   <the heart is> nourished in seas of blood coursing to and fro, and there above all is what humans call thought, because, for humans, blood around the heart does the thinking. *Porphyry*

87 (B132)   Happy the one who has gained the wealth of divine understanding, wretched he who cherishes an unenlightened opinion about the gods. *Clement*

88 (B133)   It is not possible to bring <the divine> close within reach of our eyes or to grasp him with the hands, by which the broadest path of persuasion for men leads to the mind. *Clement*

89 (B134)   He is not equipped with a human head on a body, two branches do not spring from his back, he has no feet, no swift knees, no shaggy genitals, but he is mind alone, holy and inexpressible, darting through the whole cosmos with swift thoughts. *Ammonius*

90 (B129)   And there was among them a man knowing an immense amount, who had acquired a great treasure of thoughts, master especially of all kinds of wise works; for whenever he reached out with all his thoughts, easily he saw each of the things that there are, in ten and even twenty human generations. *Porphyry*

91 (B110)   If you push them firmly under your crowded thoughts, and contemplate them favourably with unsullied and constant attention, assuredly all these will be with you through life, and you will gain much else from them, for of themselves they will cause each thing to grow into the character, according to the nature of each. But if you yourself shall reach out for the countless trivialities which come among men and dull their meditations, straightaway these will leave you as the time comes round, longing to reach their own familiar kind; for know that all things have consciousness and a share of intelligence. *Hippolytus*

92 (B111)   You will learn remedies for ills and help against old age, since for you alone shall I accomplish all these things. You will check the force of tireless winds which sweep over land and destroy fields with their blasts; and again, if you wish, you will restore compensating breezes. After black rain you will bring dry weather in season for men, and too after summer dryness you will bring tree-nourishing showers from the air, and you will lead from Hades the life-force of a dead man. *Diogenes, Clement*

Purifications

93 (B112)   My friends, living by the yellow river in the great town of Acragas, on the city's citadel, you who care for good deeds (havens of kindness for strangers, with no experience of misfortune), greetings! I travel up and down among you like an immortal god, mortal no longer, as it seems, honoured by all and crowned with ribbons and fresh garlands. Whenever I enter prosperous towns I am revered by both men and women. They follow me in countless numbers, to find out where their advantage lies, some seeking prophecies, others, long pierced by harsh pains, ask to hear the word of healing for all kinds of illnesses. *Diogenes, Clement*

94 (B114)   My friends, I know that there is truth in the words which I shall speak, but it is very difficult for men, and the onrush of conviction to the mind is unwelcome. *Clement*

95 (B11)   Fools, for their meditations have not far-reaching thoughts, men who suppose that what formerly did not exist comes into existence, or that something dies and is completely destroyed. *Plutarch*

96 (B113)   But why do I lay stress on this, as if it were some great achievement of mine, if I am superior to human mortals, constantly dying? *Sextus*

97 (B15)   A man who is wise in such matters would not surmise in his mind that men are, and good and ill befall them, for a lifetime as they call it, and that before they were formed, and after they have disintegrated, they do not exist at all. *Plutarch*

98 (B115)   There is a decree of necessity, ratified long ago by gods, eternal and sealed by broad oaths, that whenever anyone from fear defiles his own limbs in error, having mistakenly made false the oath he swore – *daimo¯nes* to whom life long-lasting is apportioned – he wanders from the blessed ones for three times ten thousand years, being born throughout the time as all kinds of mortal forms, exchanging one hard way of life for another. For the force of air pursues him into sea, and sea spits him out on to earth's surface, earth casts him into the rays of the blazing sun and sun into the eddies of air; one takes him from another and all abhor him. I too am now one of these, an exile from the gods and a wanderer, having put my trust in raging strife. *Hippolytus, Plutarch, Plotinus*

99 (B117)   For before now I have been at some time boy and girl, bush, bird and a mute fish in the sea. *Hippolytus*

100 (B116)   <She> abhors intolerable necessity. *Plutarch*

101(B126)   [...] enclosing in an unfamiliar tunic of flesh [...]. *Plutarch*

102 (B119)   [...] from honour and height of happiness [...]. *Plutarch*

103 (B118)   [...] I wept and wailed on seeing an unfamiliar place[...]. *Clement*

104 (B121/142/153a)   [A] joyless place, where there is slaughter and death and hatred, and parching fevers and consumptions and dropsy; they wander in darkness over the field of Ate [...] the house of aegis-bearing Zeus does not receive him nor the house of Hades [...] a baby grown in seven months. *Hierocles, Proclus, Herculaneum, Theo of Smyrna*

105 (B124)   Alas, wretched unhappy race of mortals, from what strifes and lamentations were you born. *Clement*

106 (B120)   We have come under this roofed cavern. *Porphyry*

107 (B122)   There were earth and far-seeing sun, bloody discord and serene harmony, beauty and ugliness, speed and slowness, lovely truth and blind uncertainty. *Plutarch*

108 (B123)   Birth and death, sleep and wakefulness, movement and rest, much-crowned splendour and ignominy, silence and speech. *Cornutus*

109 (B128)   They did not have Ares as god or Cydoimos, nor Zeus as king nor Cronos nor Poseidon, but Cypris was queen. Her they propitiated with holy images and painted animal figures, with perfumes of subtle fragrance and offerings of distilled myrrh and sweet-smelling frankincense, and pouring on the earth libations of golden honey. Their altar was not drenched by the unspeakable slaughter of bulls, but this was the greatest defilement among the people – to deprive of life and consume noble limbs. *Porphyry*

110 (B130)   All creatures – animals and birds – were tame and gentle to humans, and bright was the flame of their friendship. *Scholiast*

111 (B139)   Alas that the pitiless day did not first destroy me, before I devised for my lips the cruel deed of eating flesh. *Porphyry*

112 (B135)   [B]ut the law for all extends throughout wide-ruling air and measureless sunlight. *Aristotle*

113 (B136)   Will you not cease from the din of slaughter? Do you not see that, in your careless way of thinking, you are devouring one another? *Sextus*

114 (B145)   That is why, distraught with bitter misfortunes, you will never lighten your hearts of grievous sorrows. *Clement*

115 (B137)   The father will lift up his dear son in a changed form, and, blind fool, as he prays he will slay him, and those who take part in the sacrifice bring <the victim> as he pleads. But the father, deaf to his cries, slays him in his house and prepares an evil feast. In the same way son seizes father, and children their mother, and having deprived them of life devour the flesh of those they love. *Sextus*

116 (B138)   [...] drawing off life with bronze [...]. *Plutarch*

117 (B140)   Keep completely from leaves of laurel. *Plutarch*

118 (B141)   Wretches, utter wretches, keep your hands from beans. *Didymus*

119 (B125)   [F]or from living creatures it set out dead bodies. *Clement*

120 (B127)   Among animals they are born as lions that make their lairs in the hills and bed on the ground, and among fair-leafed trees as laurels. *Aelian*

121 (B146)   At the end they come among men on earth as prophets, minstrels, physicians and leaders, and from these they arise as gods, highest in honour. *Clement*

122 (B147)   With other immortals they share hearth and table, having no part in human sorrows, unwearied. *Clement*

Anaxagoras of Clazomenae

1 (B1)   All things were together, unlimited in number and smallness; and even the small was unlimited, and all things being together nothing was distinct because of its smallness. For air and *aethēr* covered everything, both being unlimited. For these are the greatest in all things, both in quantity and size. *Simplicius*

2 (B2)   For air and *aethēr* are being separated out from the quantity of what surrounds, and what surrounds is unlimited in amount. *Simplicius*

3 (B3)   There is no least of what is small, but always a lesser (for it is not possible for what there is not to be); and there is always a larger than the large, and equal to the small in amount; for each thing in relation to itself is both large and small. *Simplicius*

4 (B4)   Since this is so, we must believe that there are many things of all kinds in all that is coming together and seeds of all things with all kinds of forms and colours and smells. Humans were compacted, and all the other animals that have life. And for such humans there are inhabited cities and harvested fields as with us, and they have a sun and moon and the rest like us, and their earth has much produce of all kinds, the best of which they gather in and use at home. So this is what I have said about the separating off, that there would not only be a separating off with us but elsewhere as well. Before the separating off, when all things were together, there was no colour distinct at all; for the mixture of all things was preventing it – of the wet and the dry and the hot and the cold and the bright and the dark, and the quantity of earth within and the great number of limitless seeds, not at all like each other. And none of the other things were clearly alike, one to another. Since this is so we must believe that all things are in the whole. *Simplicius*

5 (B21a)   The seen gives a glimpse of the unseen. *Sextus*

6 (B21)   Because of the weakness <of our senses> we are unable to judge the truth. *Sextus*

7 (B17)   The Greeks are not right to think that there is generation and destruction, for nothing is generated or destroyed, but there is a mixing and a separating of existing things. And so they would be right to call generation mixing and destruction separating. *Simplicius*

8 (B5)   After these have been broken up in this way we must understand that all the things that there are are neither less nor more; for it is impossible for there to be more than all things, but all things are always as many as they are. *Simplicius*

9 (B6) And since there are equal shares in quantity of the large and small, so too there would be everything in everything; for they are not separate, but everything has a portion of everything. Since there is no least it would not be possible for there to be separation, nor for anything to exist on its own, but as at the beginning so now everything is altogether. And in everything there are many things even of what is being separated off, equal in quantity in the greater and the less. *Simplicius*

10 (B7) So that it is not possible to know the quantity of what is being separated off either in theory or practice. *Simplicius*

11 (B8) The contents of the cosmos are not separated from each other or cut off by an axe – not the hot from the cold nor the cold from the hot. *Simplicius*

12 (B10) How could hair come from what is not hair and flesh from what is not flesh? *Scholiast*

13 (B11) In everything there is a portion of everything except of mind [*nous*], but some have mind as well. *Simplicius*

14 (B12)

i Other things have a portion of everything, but mind is unlimited, self-determining, and mixed with no thing; it alone has independent existence. For if it were not independent, but mixed with some other thing, it would have a share in all things, if it had been mixed with any one; for there is a portion of everything in everything, as I said earlier. And what was mixed with it would prevent it from controlling any one thing in the way that it does by being alone and independent.

ii It is the most rarefied of all things and the purest, and has knowledge of each thing, and the greatest power. All that has life, whether larger or smaller, mind controls, and mind controlled the rotation of the whole, so as to make it rotate in the beginning. First it began the rotation from a small area, now it brings more into the rotation, and will bring even more.

iii Mind knew all that had been mixed and was being separated and becoming distinct. And all that was going to be, all that was but is no longer, and all that is now and will be, mind arranged in order, and this rotation too, in which now rotate the stars and sun and moon and air and *aethēr*, as they are being separated off. And it was the rotation that caused the separation. The dense is being separated off from the rare, and the hot from the cold, the bright from the dark and the dry from the wet.

iv   But there are many portions of many things, and no thing is completely separated or distinct from another except mind. Mind is all the same, whether larger or smaller. Nothing else is like any one thing, but each individual object most obviously is and was what that object has most of. *Simplicius*

15 (B13)   And when mind initiated movement there was a separating off from all that was being moved, and all that mind moved was made distinct; and the rotation of what was being moved and made distinct was causing much more to be made distinct. *Simplicius*

16 (B14)   And mind, which ever exists, is certainly even now with everything else, in the periphery and in what has come together and in what has been separated off. *Simplicius*

17 (B15)   The thick and the wet and the cold and the dark came together, and there now is earth; the fine and the hot and the dry moved out towards the furthest part of the *aethēr*. *Simplicius*

18 (B16)   From these, as they were separating off, earth was compacted; for water is separated off from the clouds, and from water earth, and from earth stones are compacted by the cold. *Simplicius*

19 (B18)   The sun gives its brightness to the moon. *Plutarch*

20 (B19)   We call Iris the light in the clouds facing the sun. So it is the sign of a storm, for the moisture encircling the cloud causes a gale or pours down as rain. *Scholiast*

Leucippus and Democritus

1 (67B2)   Leucippus says in his *On Mind*: "nothing happens in vain, but everything according to reason and from necessity." *Aetius*

2 (68B116)   Democritus: I came to Athens and no one recognised me. *Diogenes*

3 (B118)   Democritus used to say that he would rather make one discovery for which he could give the reason than be king of the Persians. *Eusebius*

Knowledge

4 (B117)   In fact we know nothing, for truth is deep down. *Diogenes*

5 (B165)   Man is all that we know. *Sextus*

6 (B8) It will be obvious that it is impossible to understand what each thing is in reality. *Sextus*

7 (B7) This reasoning shows that in truth we know nothing about anything, but opinion for each of us is an inflowing. *Sextus*

8 (B9) By convention sweet and bitter, by convention hot and cold, by convention colour, but in reality atoms and void. [...] In reality we know nothing for certain, but there is change according to the condition of the body and of what enters it and comes up against it. *Sextus*

9 (B11) There are two kinds of knowing – the genuine and the bastard. Seeing, hearing, smell, taste and touch all belong to the 'bastard' kind, but the genuine is set apart from these. *Sextus*

10 (B125) Wretched mind – after getting your evidence from us, you throw us down; but the throw brings you down with us. *Sextus*

Atomism

11 (A6) Leucippus and his associate Democritus spoke of 'the full' and 'the empty' as elements, calling the one – the full and solid – 'what is,' and the other – the empty– 'what is not,' and that is why they say that what is *is* no more than what is not, and that 'empty' is as real as body. *Aristotle*

12 (A14) <Leucippus and Democritus> said that the first principles are unlimited in number; they thought that they were 'atoms,' indivisible and incapable of being acted on because they are 'packed' and contain no parts of void, for division occurs where there is void in bodies. These atoms differ in shape, size, position and arrangement, and are separated from each other in the unlimited void. They move in the void, and, when they overtake each other, they collide – some rebound in whatever direction they happen to be, but others become entangled one with another because of their shape, size, position and arrangement and stay together, and that is how the generation of compounds results. *Simplicius*

13 (A1) Worlds are generated in the following way. Many bodies [i.e. atoms] of all sorts of shapes are 'cut off' from the infinite and move into a great void. There they come together and produce a 'whirling,' in which they collide with one another and revolve in different ways and begin to separate out, like to like. But when there are so many that they can no longer rotate in equilibrium, those that are fine go to the surrounding void as if 'sifted,' while the rest stay together and become entangled, and, while they move together, they form a spherical structure. It is like a 'membrane' which contains all sorts of bodies, and, as the atoms, packed

together, keep flowing round in the whirl, the centre solidifies and the surrounding membrane thins out. So the earth is formed when the atoms that had been brought to the middle stay together there, while the surrounding membrane expands as it attracts bodies from outside, drawing in whatever it touches as it whirls around. Some that get entangled form a structure that is at first moist and muddy, but, as they revolve with the whirling of the whole, they dry out and ignite to form the substance of the stars. *Diogenes*

14 (B167) A whirl of all kinds of forms was separated off from the whole. *Simplicius*

15 (B164) Animals join others of their same kind – doves with doves and cranes with cranes, and likewise with other non-rational forms of life. This is the case too even with lifeless things, as you can see with seeds that have been sieved and pebbles on the beach. In the former example the circular movement of the sieve sorts out lentils to go with lentils, barley with barley and wheat with wheat, and in the latter oval pebbles are pushed by the tidal wave to the same place as other oval pebbles, and round ones to go with round, as if their very similarity brought them together. *Sextus*

16 (B34) [...] in man, who is a cosmos in miniature, according to Democritus. *David*

The cone puzzle

17 (B155) This is the puzzle which Democritus set out in a scientific way: If a cone were sliced by a plane parallel to the base what should we think about the surfaces of the segments – are they equal or unequal? If they are unequal, the cone will have many indentations, like steps, and be uneven; but if the surfaces are equal the segments will be equal, and the cone will obviously have the properties of a cylinder, since all the circular slices will not be unequal but of the same size. *Plutarch*

Ethics

18 (B33) Nature and education are similar, for education re-forms a man, and in the process of re-forming sets the nature.

19 (B242) More are good as a result of practice than because of their nature.

20 (B241) Continuous hard work becomes easier as you get used to it.

21 (B184)   Continuously keeping company with worthless people increases the condition of vice.

22 (B158)   Having a new thought every day. *Plutarch*

23 (B170)   Happiness is of the soul, as is unhappiness. *Simplicius*

24 (B171)   Soul the home of *daimōn*. *Simplicius*

25 (A101)   Democritus: soul and mind are the same. *Aristotle*

26 (B181)   By doing right from understanding and knowledge one becomes simultaneously brave and straight-thinking. *Stobaeus*

27 (B182)   Learning achieves fine things through effort, but what is shameful comes automatically, without effort. *Stobaeus*

28 (B180)   Education is an adornment in good fortune and a sanctuary in misfortune. *Stobaeus*

29 (B216)   Untroubled wisdom is worth everything, being most honoured. *Stobaeus*

30 (B197)   Foolish men are formed by chance gifts, but those who understand such things by the gifts of wisdom. *Stobaeus*

31 (B31)   Medicine heals diseases of the body, whereas wisdom frees the soul from emotions. *Clement*

Serenity

32 (A1)   The aim is serenity, which is not the same as pleasure, as some have mistakenly supposed, but a calm and stable state of soul, in which it is not disturbed by any fear or superstition or any other emotion. He also calls it 'well-being' and by many other names. *Diogenes*

33 (B174)   The serene man, doing what is just and lawful, waking and sleeping is glad and strong and carefree. *Stobaeus*

34 (B189)   It is best for a man to live his life as serenely as possible and with the least distress. *Stobaeus*

35 (B3)   Anyone who intends to be serene should not busy himself with much, either in private or public. *Plutarch*

36 (B191)   Serenity comes to people from moderation in pleasure and harmony in life. *Stobaeus*

37 (B146)   Accustomed to find joy in oneself. *Stobaeus*

38 (B247)   The wise man can walk the whole earth, for the entire cosmos is the homeland of the good soul. *Stobaeus*

Appendix B

The Presocratic Sources

Not even a single work survives from the early Greek philosophers. Modern scholarship aims to reconstruct Presocratic thought through ancient sources. The ancient authors who refer directly or indirectly to early Greek thinkers extend in time from Hippias of Elis in the fifth century BCE to the Neoplatonic Simplicius in the sixth century CE, and even to the Byzantine poet and grammarian Ioannis Tzetzes (*c.* 1110–1180). Fragments and testimonia of Presocratic accounts can be found in ancient authors such as Plato (427–347 BCE), Aristotle (384–322 BCE), Theophrastus (*c.* 371–*c.* 287 BCE), Plutarch (*c.* 50–120 CE), Diogenes Laertius (*fl.* early third century CE), Hippolytus (*c.* 170–*c.* 236 CE), Stobaeus (*fl.* fifth century CE) and Simplicius (*fl. c.* 530 CE). A network of **doxography** including reports, summaries and paraphrases of Presocratic accounts, found particularly in authors of late antiquity, is also an invaluable source. Presocratic materials can be also traced to ancient dictionaries such as Hesychius' *Alphabetical Collection of All Words* (*c.* fifth century CE) and the *Etymologicum magnum*, a lexicon/encyclopedia compiled by an unknown Byzantine lexicographer in Constantinople around 1150 CE.

> **doxography**
>
> tenets of ancient accounts or opinions (*doxaî*), usually preserved in past authors

Introduction to Presocratics: A Thematic Approach to Early Greek Philosophy with Key Readings, First Edition. Giannis Stamatellos.
© 2012 John Wiley & Sons, Inc. Published 2012 by John Wiley & Sons, Inc.

The sophists Hippias of Elis (fifth century BCE) and Gorgias of Leontinoi (*c*. 483–*c*. 376 BCE) seem to be the first thinkers to offer collections of Presocratic accounts. Whereas Hippias aimed to reconcile earlier thinkers and accounts, Gorgias aimed to refute and criticize precedent theories. Plato (429–347 BCE) referred to the Presocratics, particularly the Ionians and the Eleatics. Aristotle (384–322 BCE) treated the Presocratic accounts as 'reputable opinions' (*endoxa*), which had to be discussed in philosophical dialogue and made to contribute to the dialectics of divergent views and to the exploration of truth. Theophrastus (*c*. 371–*c*. 287 BCE), a colleague and successor of Aristotle in the Lyceum, collected, in his *Physical Opinions*, various accounts of the Presocratic philosophers (and other predecessors) on the philosophy of nature. Theophrastus divided his work into 16 (or 18) books, organized thematically, by topics. His aim was to refute false doctrines on nature and to justify valid ones in the light of Aristotle's physics and metaphysics. However, only the last book *On Sensation* is extant, while extracts survive from the first book *On Material Principles*. Theophrastus' *Physical Opinions* seems to have been the principal source for Presocratic doxography in antiquity. Aetius, an unknown compiler of the first century CE, put together his *Placita* – a summary of Theophrastus' *Opinions*, reconstructed by Hermann Diels in *Doxographi Graeci* (1879) – by using pseudo-Plutarch's *Placita*, Stobaeus *Anthology* and a work of the fifth-century CE Christian bishop Theodoret, entitled *Therapy of Greek Diseases*.

Diogenes Laertius (*fl.* third century CE), in his *Lives of Philosophers*, reports significant biographical information about eminent Greek philosophers, from the Seven Sages to Epicurus. John Stobaeus (*fl.* fifth century CE), in his four-book *Anthologium*, offers a compilation of quotations from ancient authors. Stobaeus emphasizes ethical sayings that serve an educative purpose. Plutarch (*c*. 50–120 CE) also focuses on ethical issues in his *Moralia*, making extensive references to, and giving quotations from, the Presocratics. Sextus Empiricus (*fl.* late second century CE), a Skeptic philosopher and physician, quotes extensively from early Greek thinkers, particularly in the seventh and ninth book of his *Adversus mathematicos*.

Hippolytus of Rome (*c*. 170–*c*. 236 CE) was a Christian theologian who compiled a *Refutation of All Heresies* that contains refutations of pagan accounts, including the Presocratics, and particularly Heraclitus. Despite the polemic character of his work, the *Refutations* should be considered as an important source for early Greek philosophers. Clement of Alexandria (died *c.* 215 CE) was a convert to Christianity who had a thorough knowledge of Greek literature. In his *Protrepticus* and *Stromateis* (or *Miscellanies*) he compares paganism and Christianity by making reference to ancient Greek authors, including the Presocratics.

In *Praeparatio evangelica* (X.3.468), Eusebius of Caesarea (*c.* 263–339 CE) claimed that the books of Plato's predecessors were "rare to find." However, three centuries later, at the beginning of the sixth century CE, the Neoplatonic philosopher and scholar Simplicius (*fl. c.* 530 CE) offered a significant amount of Presocratic fragments (particularly from Parmenides' poem) and testimonies in his commentaries on Aristotle's *Physics* and *De caelo*. Simplicius' source in the *Physics* commentary was mainly Theophrastus, via the Peripatetic Alexander of Aphrodisias (*fl.* late second to early third century CE) and his lost commentary on Aristotle's *Physics*. Simplicius, through Alexander and Theophrastus, recognized Aristotle's contribution to the study of early Greek philosophers. Simplicius seems to be aware of the 'rarity' of the Presocratic texts and of the kinds of threat to pagan sources that were common in his period. Simplicius' testimony is invaluable for the study of early Greek philosophers, not only because it preserves the original texts, but also because it interprets the Presocratic accounts through a Neoplatonic perspective. The Neoplatonic interest in Presocratic philosophy can also be traced back to Plotinus' *Enneads* in the third century CE). Presocratic elements can equally be found in eminent Neoplatonists such as Porphyry (*c.* 234–*c.* 305 CE), Iamblichus (*c.* 250–325 CE) and Proclus (*c.* 410-485 CE).

Other important sources of the Presocratics are the Epicurean Philodemus of Gadara (*c.* 110–*c.* 40 BCE); the Stoics Arius Didymus (first century BCE to first century CE) and Marcus Aurelius (121–180 CE); the eclectic philosopher Maximus Tyrius of the second century CE; the Christian Origen of Alexandria (185–232 CE); the Aristotelian commentators Themistius (*fl. c.* 390 CE) and Ammonius (*fl. c.* 500 CE); and Numenius of Apamea, a Platonist philosopher of the second century CE.

Further Reading

Mansfeld, J. (1999) "Sources," in Long (ed.), 22–44.
Runia, T. D. (2008) "The Sources for Presocratic Philosophy," in Curd and Graham (eds.), 27–54.

Appendix C

The Presocratic Legacy

The following list of authors and schools provides only a brief historical outline of the Presocratic reception and legacy. The list is not exhaustive but selective. It aims to show the importance of the Presocratics by indicating their use in later traditions and schools.

The Playwrights

Presocratic ideas have been integrated into the plays of the tragic poets Aeschylus (c. 525–456 BCE), Sophocles (c. 496–406 BCE) and Euripides (c. 480–406 BCE) and of the comic play writer Aristophanes (c. 446–386 BCE). Euripides refers to early Greek philosophers when he congratulates those who learned the "art of inquiry" on the origins and "ageless order of immortal nature" (fr. 190). Presocratic cosmological patterns can be detected in Euripides' lost *Wise Melanippe* and in Aeschylus' *Danaids*, while in the *Oresteia* Aeschylus conceives of the cycles of events as a unity of opposites that reflects Heraclitus and Empedocles. Euripides (in *Heracles* and *Ion*) and Aeschylus (in fr. 350) adopted Presocratic criticisms – particularly of Xenophanes, Heraclitus and Empedocles – about the immoral behavior of the anthropomorphic gods. Sophocles' unknowable nature of the divine in *Oedipus the King* echoes Xenophanes' and Parmenides' doubts about mortal beliefs, while Aristophanes' *Clouds* was not only a comic portrait of Socrates but also a parody of early Greek philosophers such as Anaxagoras, who wondered on meteorological phenomena.

Introduction to Presocratics: A Thematic Approach to Early Greek Philosophy with Key Readings, First Edition. Giannis Stamatellos.
© 2012 John Wiley & Sons, Inc. Published 2012 by John Wiley & Sons, Inc.

Plato

Plato (427–347 BCE) was critical of some Presocratics, often mentioning them indirectly. On the one hand he criticized Heraclitus and some Heracliteans such as Cratylus (*Theaetetus* 181a1 ff.), and he was ironic with the 'Ionian and Sicilian Muses' in the *Sophist* (242c8–243a4). On the other hand, he acknowledged Parmenides as 'great' (*Sophist* 237a4– 5), 'revered' and 'awe-inspiring (*Theaetetus* 183e ff.). For Plato, Parmenides, along with Melissus, is the Presocratic who appropriately supported the unity and immobility of being (*Theaetetus* 180e ff.; *Sophist* 237a ff.). Nevertheless, in other cases Plato harmonizes contradictory Presocratic accounts. For instance, in the cosmogonical narrative of the *Timaeus*, Eleatic, Pythagorean and Ionian theories are used in Plato's ontological synthesis of being and becoming. Moreover, Plato's theory of the Forms could be regarded as a synthesis between Heraclitus' flux of becoming and the Eleatic eternal stability of being. Recent studies further enlighten Plato's use of the Presocratics.

Aristotle

Aristotle (384–322 BCE) was critical of 'natural philosophers' (*phusiologoi*), and his view of the Presocratics influenced our modern view of these early Greek thinkers. Aristotle considered it important for his own philosophy to examine the views of his predecessors. However, he tended to see the Presocratics as taking faltering steps towards the goal he had reached and to interpret their ideas in terms of his own philosophy and terminology. For instance, he criticized Heraclitus' theory of flux and the unity of opposites in terms of the law of non-contradiction. Nevertheless, it has to be noted that Aristotle explored systematically Presocratic questions such as causation (*Metaphysics* A), the soul (*De anima*), physical change and time (*Physics*), elements and matter (*De generatione et corruptione*).

The Hellenistic Age

The Hellenistic schools adapted various aspects of Presocratic physics and ethics. In Stoic physics the principle of life is a 'living spirit' or 'breath' (*pneuma*), a hot, breath-like fiery substance, like Heraclitus' fire.

For the Stoics, the universe as a whole is a living organism constructed by the *pneuma*. This fiery force is an eternal and divine formative principle (*logos*), the ruling and ordering principle of the universe, which constructs the material world according to a divine plan. Epicurus (341–271 BCE) followed Democritus, but he introduced important differences in atomic theory and in ethics. Epicurus claimed that there is no moving cause and no ordering intelligence; and he denied divine activity. All things are simply chance collections of atoms coming together and separating off in the void. Many worlds are simultaneously possible and the void, like the number and the shapes of atoms, is infinite. The Roman poet Lucretius (99 or 94 to 55 BCE), a contemporary of Cicero, presents Epicurean atomic doctrines and argument in epic hexameters (a poetic form following Parmenides and Empedocles) in his Latin poem *On the Nature of Things*. This work emphasized atomic theory and the criticisms of opponents (Books 1–2), as well as the structure of the soul and the arguments for its mortality (Book 3). For Lucretius, atomic theory signified freedom from fears about the gods' interference in our lives and about punishment after death.

Neopythagoreanism

In the second century CE a genuine rebirth of the Pythagorean tradition came with the movement known as Neopythagoreanism. The key concepts of Neopythagoreanism were the divine perfection of the Monad, expressed in a hierarchy of numbers, and the immortality of the soul. Nicomachus of Gerasa (*c.* 150 CE) and his *Theological Arithmetic* – a mystical work that includes a metaphysical identification of numbers with the traditional gods – should be regarded as the starting point for this Neopythagorean revival. Moderatus (*fl. c.* 90 CE) and Numenius (*fl. c.* 150 CE) were influential figures of Neopythagoreanism.

Late Antiquity

In late antiquity, from around 250 until about 750 CE, Presocratic thought was influential in relation to Neoplatonism – a later development of Plato's philosophical teaching. Plotinus (204–270 CE), the principal Neoplatonic figure, refers by name to some of the main Presocratic philosophers such as Heraclitus, Parmenides, Empedocles and Anaxagoras. In the *Enneads* Plotinus treats early Greek philosophers as independent thinkers. He considers them to be pre-Platonists who contributed to the development of the Greek philosophical tradition. Presocratic concepts can be found in key areas of Plotinus' thought such as the One, Intellect and Being; Eternity and Time; Soul and Matter. The influence of the Presocratics can also be detected in the thought of later Neoplatonists like Porphyry (*c*. 232–*c*. 305 CE), Iamblichus (died *c*. 326 CE) and Proclus (412–385 CE). It is noteworthy that one of the most important late sources for the Presocratics is the Neoplatonic philosopher and scholar Simplicius (*c*. 490–560 CE).

The Middle Ages

In the Middles Ages copies of Anaxagoras' book and of some poems of Empedocles were extant in the Eastern Roman Empire; they were used by Byzantine scholars. In Islamic theosophical literature sporadic references and allusions of eminent Presocratics such as Heraclitus and Empedocles can be found with reference to the Neoplatonists. For instance, in the *Theology of Aristotle* (an Arabic translation, paraphrase and commentary of Plotinus' *Enneads* IV–VI, falsely attributed to Aristotle) the adaptor interprets Empedocles in the light of Plotinus' theory of the soul.

The Renaissance

In the Renaissance the Presocratic philosophers became known indirectly, probably through the Platonic and the Aristotelian corpus. Pletho (*c*. 1360–*c*. 1450) inspired Cosimo de' Medici to found the Platonic Academy of Florence, where Marsilio Ficino (1433–1499) composed a Latin translation of Plato, published in 1484, and the first Latin translation and commentary of Plotinus' *Enneads*, completed in 1490 and printed in 1492. Ficino also showed a particular interest in occult science and religion. Among other works Ficino translated the Orphic and Homeric Hymns, Hesiod's *Theogony*, parts of the Hermetic Corpus and the *Golden Thoughts* of Pythagoras.

Presocratic trends can be also found in Nicholas Cusanus (1401–1464). His principle of the 'coincidence of contraries' seems to echo the unity of opposites found in Heraclitus and Empedocles. Giordano Bruno

(1548–1600) followed Cusanus' principle of the 'coincidence of contraries' – and particularly the coincidence of potentiality and actuality in God. Bruno's view of an infinite and homogenous universe can be traced back to the Presocratics, and various direct references to eminent Presocratics can be found in his work. The philosophy of Cusanus and Bruno, along with medieval occult science, marked a starting point for Renaissance Platonism, which was later reflected in the work of many innovators such as Paracelsus (1493–1541).

The Scientific Revolution

The seventeenth century scientific revolution, started by Copernicus (1473–1543), Galileo Galilei (1564–1642), Kepler (1571–1630) and Newton (1643–1727), is characterized by a denial of Aristotelianism and by a revival of Platonic, Pythagorean and atomic philosophy. In particular, the German mathematician and astronomer Johannes Kepler, in *Mysterium Cosmographicum* (1621), was fascinated by Pythagoras' mathematics and *musica universalis*. Likewise, Francis Bacon in *Novum Organum* recognizes most of the Presocratics as forerunners of natural philosophy and experimentation – people who searched for the truth with discipline and modesty.

Modern Philosophy

The French philosopher and mathematician René Descartes (1596–650) is regarded as the father of modern philosophy and, along with Baruch Spinoza (1632–1677) and Gottfried Leibniz (1646–1716), as one of the most distinguished figures of continental rationalism. The Cartesian *cogito* could be conceived of as the *reverse* of the ontological priority between the thinking subject and the thinking object in Parmenides' *thinking* (B3): whereas the Parmenidean subject grasps reality *objectively*, through thinking (*noein*), the Cartesian subject cognizes reality *subjectively*, in self-reflection (*cogito*). Berkeley's thesis *esse est percipi (aut percipere)* — "to be is to be perceived (or to perceive)" – could also be seen as another inroad made by the Parmenidean theory of being.

The Dutch philosopher Baruch de Spinoza (1632–1677) was attracted to the Eleatic Zeno and his paradoxes of motion. In *The Principles of Cartesian Philosophy*, published in Amsterdam in 1663, Spinoza maintained that Zeno's paradoxes rest on false prejudices, caused by an erroneous conception of matter and time (Part 2, Proposition 6). Matter in Spinoza's argument is infinitely extended and ontologically unified ("the matter of the heavens and the earth is one and the same"), and time is also infinitely divisible in the duration of motion ("time is the measure of motion"). Spinoza emphatically supports the rational justification of his solution: "I opposed Zeno's reasonings with my reasonings, and so I have refuted him by reason, not by the senses [...]." (Part 2, Proposition 6). Moreover, Spinoza praises Thales of Miletus (Letter 44, 17 February 1671) for the excellence of his reflections on human friendship, wisdom and good life. Spinoza's source is probably the fifteenth-century Latin translation of Diogenes Laertius.

Georg W. F. Hegel

In the eighteenth century the German philosopher Georg W. F. Hegel (1770–1831) showed a special interest in Parmenides and Heraclitus. In his *Lectures on the History of Philosophy*, Hegel declared that "there is no proposition of Heraclitus which I have not adopted in my logic." Although he was ready to admit that philosophy began with Parmenides, he understood that Heraclitus was the first to recognize dialectic as the principle of all contradictions. Hegel recognized *to hen* (the one) as the key word of Parmenides and *logos* as the key word of Heraclitus. For Hegel, Heraclitus' importance lies in the understating of the nature of infinity that includes the inherent contradictory negativity of reality in which 'being' and 'nothingness' are mere empty abstractions. In the Hegelian perspective, Heraclitus' time reflects an immanent dialectical opposition that appears in the everlasting flux of becoming.

Karl Marx

Karl Marx (1818–1883) and Fredrick Engels (1820–1895) considered Heraclitus to be a forerunner of dialectical materialism for his concept of development through the conflict of opposites. Karl Marx was educated in ancient Greek literature, and it is noteworthy that his doctoral dissertation *The Difference between the Democritean and Epicurean Philosophy of Nature* (written in 1841, published in 1902) compared and evaluated the physical theories of Democritus and Epicurus.

Friedrich Nietzsche

In the late nineteenth century Friedrich Nietzsche (1844–1900) expressed enthusiastic admiration for the early Greek thinkers. From 1872 to 1876 – a few years before Diels' publication of *Doxographi Graeci* in 1879 – Nietzsche lectured on the 'pre-Platonic philosophers' in the University of Basel. At this early stage of his career, Nietzsche used the term 'pre-Platonics' to refer to the Presocratics and Socrates, just as in his *Philosophy in the Tragic Age of the Greeks* he speaks of the "Republic of geniuses from Thales to Socrates." However, in *The Birth of Tragedy* Nietzsche criticizes Socrates and the sophists as enemies of the tragic age of Greece. He regards the Presocratics, in contrast to the philosophers who came after Socrates, as "the crown of the golden age" of ancient Greek philosophy. These early philosophers balanced passion and action in life in a harmonious synthesis of the Dionysian and the Apollonian spirit. In his *Philosophy in the Tragic Age of the Greeks*, Nietzsche promoted the view that Thales' assertion that "water is the origin of all things" is important for three reasons: (1) it makes a statement about the primal origin of all things; (2) it uses language that has nothing to do with fable or myth; and (3) it reflects the vision that all things are really one. For Nietzsche, Thales used creative imagination and analogy in place of myth, as well as allegory and logical proof, to understand the common property of all things. Moreover, Nietzsche regarded Anaximander as the first thinker who attributed a moral value to existence. Compared with the primordial totality and completeness of the *apeiron*, every existence is unjust, with no value in itself, and so every individual and definite being has to pay the price by returning to the unlimited source.

The Anglo-American Tradition

In the Anglo-American tradition, W. K. C. Guthrie (1906–1981) devoted two volumes of his *History of Greek Philosophy* (1962, 1965) to the Presocratics. Earlier on, F. M. Cornford (1874–1943), his predecessor in Cambridge, had emphasized the anthropological and religious elements of the Presocratic tradition in his work *From Religion to Philosophy*. Aristotle's reading of the Presocratics was first challenged by William A. Heidel and Harold Cherniss in the early twentieth century. Heidel, in his 1906 article "Qualitative Change in Presocratic Philosophy," concentrated on a criticism of Aristotle's view of Presocratic theories of matter, while Harold Cherniss, in his book *Aristotle's Criticism of Presocratic Philosophy* (1936), questioned Aristotle's interpretation of Presocratic theories in greater detail.

The Continental Tradition

In the continental tradition the French philosopher Gilles Deleuze (1925–1995), in his *Nietzsche and Philosophy*, describes Heraclitus as the 'tragic thinker,' the philosopher "for whom life is radically innocent and just. He understands existence on the basis of an instinct of play. He makes existence an aesthetic phenomenon rather than a moral or religious one" (p. 22). In his *Visible and the Invisible*, Maurice Merleau-Ponty (1908–1961) defines 'flesh' on Heraclitean and Empedoclean terms as "strife of the unity of opposites"; 'flesh' underlies our existential unity in the world, and we should properly describe it not in modern terms of 'matter,' 'mind' or 'substance,' but "we should need the old term 'element,' in the sense it was used to speak of water, air, earth and fire" (pp. 183–184). Another renowned French philosopher, Jacques Derrida (1930–2004), recognized the ancient roots of deconstruction and *différance* in Heraclitus' fragments. In his *Original Discussion of Différance* (1968), Derrida declared: "Yes, there is much of the ancient in what I have said. It is to Heraclitus that I refer myself in the last analysis" (p. 93).

Martin Heidegger

Martin Heidegger (1889–1976) lectured on Presocratic thinkers such as Anaximander, Heraclitus and Parmenides. In 1966/1967 a Heraclitus seminar was held at the University of Freiburg; it was organized by Martin Heidegger and Eugen Fink. For Heidegger and Fink, the understanding of Heraclitus and the Presocratics was an enormous challenge. In the opening address of the seminar Fink vividly stated: "Heraclitus' voice, like that of Python, reaches us over a thousand years. Although this thinker lived at the origin of the West, and to that extend is longest past, we have not overtaken him even now" (p. 3). In *Being and Time* Heidegger retuned to Heraclitus and Parmenides, in order to overcome the nihilism of modernity and *the forgetfulness of being*. Heidegger discovered in early Greek philosophy the unmediated experience of being – that is, the pre-ontological state of being beyond metaphysics. For Heidegger, the Presocratics speak not only about "the things themselves" (die Sache selbst), as in Husserlian phenomenology, but also – and mainly – about the 'being of beings,' in an open question of existence as presencing (Anwesen). The Presocratics are not early scientists or rational philosophers, they are thinkers who search for the un-concealment (*alētheia*) of being: *what is present in presencing.*

Modern Science and Mathematics

The Presocratic philosophers intrigued and challenged modern scientific and mathematical minds. Leibniz (1646–1716) was aware of the early atomists and, despite his criticism of their materialism, there are many parallels between early atomism and his theory of monads, as exposed in *Monadologie* (1714). For Leibniz, the monads are, at a metaphysical level, the ultimate elements of the universe – substantial forms of being – as the atoms are the ultimate material elements at a physical level. The work of the early atomists, and especially their atomic theory, as developed by Democritus, have been highly recognized by modern philosophy and science. However, ancient atomism passed into oblivion until the nineteenth-century work of John Dalton, who proposed that each chemical element is composed of immutable and indestructible atoms, which combine to form complex chemical compounds.

Zeno's paradoxes of motion puzzled great mathematical minds such as that of Bertrand Russell (1872–1970), while Albert Einstein (1879–1955) seemed to be aware of some Presocratic theories of physics – particular those of Parmenides and Heraclitus. The German theoretical physicist Werner Heisenberg (1901–1976), who brought to quantum physics the uncertainty principle, acknowledged the early Greek thinkers as the pioneers of quantum theory and science of the atom. In the fourth chapter of his *Physics and Philosophy* (1958) Heisenberg refers extensively to the Presocratics, not only to Leucippus and Democritus and the concept of the atom, but also to the Milesians, Heraclitus, Parmenides, Anaxagoras and the Pythagoreans and to their concepts of substance, becoming and plurality of being: "the idea of the smallest, indivisible ultimate building blocks of matter first came up in connection with the elaboration of the concepts of Matter, Being and Becoming which characterized the first epoch of Greek philosophy" (p. 26).

Karl Popper

In the *World of Parmenides*, Karl Popper (1902–1994) reveals his great admiration for the early Greek thinkers. He calls himself as "a lover of the beautiful story of the Presocratics" – an "amateur thinker" fascinated by the radical thought of Anaximander, Parmenides, Xenophanes and Heraclitus. Popper prefaces this collection of essays by saying:

> I hope that these essays may illustrate the thesis that all history is or should be the history of problem situations, and that in following this principle we may further our understanding of the Presocratics and other thinkers of the past. The essays also try to show the greatness of the early Greek philosophers, who gave Europe its philosophy, its science and its humanism. (viii)

Popper praises Parmenides' poetry for making him learn to look at the moon and sun with new eyes – "eyes enlightened by his poetry" – and Xenophanes for his critical epistemology. He finds in Xenophanes an anticipation of his own theory of knowledge, "according to which all our scientific theories are myths, or in the words of Xenophanes, 'woven webs of guesses'" (p. 116). However, Paul Feyerabend (1924–1994) – a student of Karl Popper – was critical of Popper's epistemology of science and of any form of universal scientific method. In *Conquest of Abundance* Feyerabend disagreed with Popper's understanding of Xenophanes' 'critical rationalism.' He represented Xenophanes as one of the Western intellectuals who treated philosophy in an unprofessional, or even humorous and satiric way: "he used epigrams, one-liners, he imitated, mocked, or repeated popular profundities to reveal their shallowness" (p. 41). Feyerabend's epistemological anarchism has a parallel in the criticism directed by Theodor Adorno (1903–1969), in *Zur Metakritik der Erkenntnistheorie*, at the philosophical epistemology and "metaphysics of existence" of Parmenides.

The Psychoanalytic Tradition

Presocratic ideas can also be found in the early period of the psychoanalytic school. Sigmund Freud (1856–1939) devotes a section to Empedocles in *Analysis Terminable and Interminable* (1937) and refers explicitly to this Presocratic as "one of the grandest and most remarkable figures in the history of Greek civilization" (p. 245). Freud understands Empedocles as the first philosopher who foreshowed the dual instinct theory of Eros and Thanatos in the dual cosmic forces of Love and Strife: "the two principles of Empedocles – Love and Strife – are, both in name and function, the same as our two primal instincts Eros and destructiveness" (p. 246). Freud also regards Empedocles as the first philosopher to ascribe to the universe the same animate principles at work in individual organisms. As the Empedoclean cosmic forces of Love and Strife unify and separate the elements, the Freudian instincts of Eros and Thanatos bring unity and disunity to being.

Carl Gustav Jung (1875–1961) showed a special interest in the Presocratics, and particularly in Heraclitus. Following Heraclitus' theory of opposites, Jung stressed the existence of a conflict of opposites in human psychology, between internal and external psychic energies. In his autobiographical work *Memory, Dreams and Reflections* Jung stated: "just as all energy proceeds from opposition, so the psyche too possesses its inner polarity, this being the indispensable prerequisite for its aliveness, as Heraclitus realized long ago [...]. Indeed this is inevitable, for, as Heraclitus says, 'Everything is flux'" (pp. 346, 351). Jung used Heraclitus to explain multiple personalities by introducing the opposition between 'introverts' (in whom energy flows concentrate inward, toward the self) and 'extroverts' (in whom energy flows run outward, toward the others and the world).

Alain Badiou (2006) discussed the use of the Presocratics made by the French psychoanalyst and psychiatrist Jacques Marie Lacan (1901–1981). Lacan praised the innocent audacity of the Presocratics in identifying the powers of discourse with the conception of being. For Lacan, the Presocratics were not the phantasm of a tradition, but the symbol of a rebellion against all traditional forms of knowledge. As he stated in *Le Séminaire* (1960–1961): "Beyond Plato, in the background, we have this attempt, grandiose in its innocence – this hope residing in the first philosophers, called physicists – of finding an ultimate grasp on the real under the guarantee of discourse, which is in the end their instrument for gauging experience" (pp. 98–99). For Lacan, Heraclitus' unity in plurality of the universal flux foreshadows the relation between identity and difference, while Empedocles' Love and Strife, as Freud observed, describe the antinomy of drives. As Badiou maintained, Lacan inscribes psychoanalysis within a destiny of thought that is determined by oppositions and divisions originally informed by the Presocratics Heraclitus and Parmenides.

Fine Arts

In the fine arts, Flemish, Dutch and Spanish painters of the sixteenth and seventeenth century have been fascinated by Heraclitus and Democritus. Heraclitus has been represented as the 'weeping philosopher,' Democritus as the 'laughing philosopher.' Heraclitus and Democritus portrayed the two tragic philosophical *personae* expressing conflict between pessimistic and optimistic attitudes in life. In 1603, Rubens (1577–1640) painted a *Heraclitus, the Crying Philosopher* and a *Democritus, the Laughing Philosopher.* The same images were depicted by another Flemish painter, Jacob Jordaens (1593–1678). The Heraclitus–Democritus contrast can also be seen in the Dutch painters Cornelisz. van Haarlem (1562–1638), Johannes Moreelse (1602–1634) and Hendrick ter Brugghen (*c.* 1588–1629). Diego Velázquez (1599–1660) painted a laughing Democritus (*c.* 1624), while Rembrandt (1606–1669) pained a self-portrait titled *Rembrandt Laughing* (*c.* 1628) and gave the alternative title *The Young Rembrandt as Democritus the Laughing Philosopher.*

Modern Literature

In the area of modern literature the Presocratics are also being attended upon. Empedocles inspired the German poet Friedrich Hölderlin (1770–1843) in *Tod des Empedokles* (*The Death of Empedocles*). The same episode underlined also the narrative of Matthew Arnold's poem *Empedocles on Etna* (1852). T. S. Eliot (1888–1965) cited Heraclitus in the preface of his *Four Quartets.* In the *New Refutation of Time,* Jorge Luis Borges (1899–1986) recalls Heraclitus for his dialectical skills in the river fragments; "for the facility with which we accept the first meaning ('The river is another') covertly imposes upon us the second meaning ('I am another') and gives us the illusion of having invented it [...]."

Glossary of Greek Terms

The following list includes the Greek terms used in this book. The glossary defines most of the terms in the Presocratic context.

aēr	air, one of the elements; damp mist
aethēr	bright blue sky above misty air; the fifth element according to Aristotle
agathos	good, brave, virtuous
agora	open market and place of assembly
aiōn	eternity; everlastingness
aitia	cause; reason; explanation
akouein	listen to
akousmatikoi	the students who 'hear' the lessons of Pythagoras
akousmata	things heard; oral aphorisms of the Pythagoreans
alētheia	truth, reality
anankē	necessity
anapnein	inhale
antichthōn	counter-earth
apeiros	without boundaries, limitless; *to apeiron* the unlimited (an indefinite material substance)
aporia	perplexity; philosophical enquiry
archē	beginning; first or primary principle (here, in ontology)
aretē	virtue, excellence
aristos	best
arithmos	number, incorporeal principle
atomon	indivisible, impossible to cut; atom; plural *atoma*
bios	life, related to way or manner of life
chaos	featureless pre-cosmic abyss; the source of everything according to Hesiod

Introduction to Presocratics: A Thematic Approach to Early Greek Philosophy with Key Readings, First Edition. Giannis Stamatellos.
© 2012 John Wiley & Sons, Inc. Published 2012 by John Wiley & Sons, Inc.

chronos	time; Chronos mythical figure usually related to Cronos
chthonie	under-earth; mythical figure usually related to Hecate
daimōn	divine spirit; divine being with long-lasting life; plural *daimōnes*
dikē	justice; *adikia* injustice
doxa	opinion, belief; plural *doxai* opinions, views or doctrines of a philosopher
endoxa	reputable opinions; usually refers to the accounts of the ancient wise
(e)on	being, what-is; *to on* what-is; *to mē on* what-is-not
epistēmē	knowledge
Erinyes	Homeric avenging deities, the dark powers of Justice
esti	is; *ouk esti* is not
ēthos	moral character, behavior, habit
eudaimonia	happiness, well-being, flourishing
euthumia	serenity
eu	well, in a good way
gaia	earth, one of the elements
gnōmai	uncritical opinions
gnosis	knowledge; *gnōthi sauton* know thyself
harmonia	fitting together, harmony between opposite tensions
Hestia	hearth of the world, the central cosmic and divine fire for the Pythagoreans
historia	investigation
hudōr	water, one of the elements
hulē	matter; a term firstly used by Aristotle as an opposite to form
isonomia	equality of opposite powers
kakos	bad or evil (denotes the absence of good)
katharsis	purification
kenos	empty; *to kenon* the void, vacuum
kosmos	order, arrangement; the derivative noun *kosmēma* means 'jewel'
kouros	young man
logos	account, reason, ratio, measure; hidden cosmic rhythm for Heraclitus; plural *logoi*
mathema	lesson
mathematikoi	the students who attended inner-circle lessons of Pythagoras

mēden	what is not; *mēden agan* nothing too much
monarchia	monarchy, rule by one power
noein	thinking; the activity of intellect in the recognition of being for Parmenides
noēma	thought
nomos	human law, custom, convention, tradition
nous	mind, intelligence, intelligent force
nun	now; moment in time; a primary temporal particle
Okeanos	mythical figure of the cosmic river
Ouranos	heaven, vault, firmament of the sky
ousia	essence
pathos	passion, suffering, passiveness
pentathlos	athlete of ancient pentathlon
philosophia	love for wisdom and knowledge
philosophos	a person who loves wisdom; plural *philosophoi*
phronēsis	practical wisdom (*phronein* means to be prudent)
phusiologoi	natural philosophers (usually with reference to the Presocratics)
phusis	natural constitution and development of things
pneuma	living spirit; hot, breath-like fiery substance
polumathia	knowing many things; assembling facts
polis	independent city state
psuchē	soul, the source of life and intelligence
pur	fire, one of the elements
rhizomata	roots; a description of the four elements used by Empedocles
sēmata	signs
Silloi	satirical poems
sophrosunē	self-control, modesty, temperance
spermata	seeds
stephanoi	cosmic garlands, crowns, bands
stoicheion	element; letter in the alphabet
taxis	order
technē	skill, craft
telos	end, purpose
tetraktus	the sum of the first four numbers; sacred symbol of the Pythagoreans
thumos	strong feeling or passion
tropai	alterations, changes, turnings
zoē	life, living force

Glossary of Philosophical Terms

This glossary includes the philosophical terms used in the book. The terms are generally defined in the early Greek philosophical context, otherwise it is specified in the parenthesis after the term. The description is brief and serves as first guidance.

ad infinitum	to infinity
aesthetics	the study of art and beauty
agent (moral)	the individual, regarded as someone capable of deliberate action
agnosticism	the view that true knowledge is unattainable to humans
anthropocentrism	the evaluation and explanation of reality in human terms
anthropomorphic	attributing human features to non-human beings such as animals, inanimate objects and divinities
antinomy	the contradictory conclusion that arises from two hypothetical syllogisms, each of which appears to be independently true, but cannot be true simultaneously with the other
antithesis	opposition to a thesis or proposition
atheism	the denial of the existence of gods or divinity
atomic intertwining	atoms forming different compounds

Introduction to Presocratics: A Thematic Approach to Early Greek Philosophy with Key Readings, First Edition. Giannis Stamatellos.
© 2012 John Wiley & Sons, Inc. Published 2012 by John Wiley & Sons, Inc.

atomic scattering	atoms rebounding in different directions
atoms	particles that are *atoma*, 'indivisible'
atomic theory (Leucippus and Democritus)	the view that everything consists of imperceptible and indivisible units of matter called atoms; the atoms and the void are the principles of everything
autonomy	personal and intellectual independence
becoming	process of coming-to-be and passing-away
being	*to (e)on*, what is
benevolence	all-goodness; usually refers to a god
causality	the relation between cause and effect; the idea that every effect has a specific cause
***cogito ergo sum* (Descartes)**	"I think, therefore I am"
coincidence of contraries (Cusanus)	the claim that God is the coincidence of infinite active potency and infinite passive potency and that the maximum and the minimum of something coincide
conflict of opposites (Jung)	the inner polarity of human psyche; the conflict between introvert and extrovert psychic energies
conglomeration (Democritus)	synthesis of heterogeneous things
cosmic cycle (Empedocles)	endless recurring periods in the universe
cosmogony	the study of the origins of the universe
cosmology	the study of the nature and structure of the universe
deconstruction (Derrida)	critical theory that exposes the inner contradictions of an artwork, beyond its obvious meanings
deus ex machina	god from the machine, i.e. from a theatrical device that allowed divine characters to appear on stage as if by miracle; a supreme agent (or God) provides an unexpected solution to an unsolved problem
dialectic (Hegel)	the process by which a thing (thought or object) necessarily changes into its contradictory opposite; in Hegelian dialectic a thesis leads to an antithesis in order to arrive at a new synthesis

dialectical materialism (Marx/Engels)	the thesis that social progress occurs through conflict and struggle between economic classes
didactic ethics	branch of ethics that emphasizes instruction and education
différance **(Derrida)**	the idea that words include the internal ambiguity of 'to defer' and 'to differ'
doxography	tenets of ancient accounts or opinions (*doxai*), usually preserved in past authors
dualism	the idea that reality consists of two opposing principles or elements (e.g. the opposition between mind and body)
dynamism	power; strength; force or ability to change things
eclecticism	synthesis of theories and ideas from a variety of earlier philosophies
effluence (Democritus)	the theory that the sense organ is contracted by the sensory image emitted by the sense object (e.g. the perception of sight occurs when the visual image of an object is reflected on the eyes)
element	simple, primordial substance
empiricism	the claim that sense experience is the main source of knowledge
endless recurrence	eternal return of the same course of events
epistemology	theory of knowledge; the study of human cognition
equilibrium	balance arising from opposing forces
Erinyes	Homeric avenging deities, the dark powers of Justice
Eros and Thanatos (Freud)	the two primal Freudian instincts; Eros corresponds to unity and love; Thanatos corresponds to disunity and destruction
esse est percipi (aut percipere) **(Berkeley)**	"to be is to be perceived (or to perceive)"
eternity	endless continuation of time, without beginning or end
ethics	the systematic study of morality, involving questions of human behavior or conduct and what is considered to be right and wrong in particular

cases; from the Greek *ethos* (character/custom/disposition)

existence (Eleatic)   what actually is

flesh   the existential intertwining of the perceiver and
(Merleau-Ponty)   the perceived; an elemental matrix of interaction
between subject and object in the web of life

flux   the idea that everything is in constant change and
mobility

force   something that changes the condition of things

geocentric   which considers earth as the centre of the cosmos
(said of a cosmological model)

geostatic   which considers the earth as static or immovable
(said of a cosmological model)

Great Year   the period of time during which all the planets
return to the same configuration

heroic ethics   ethics that promotes heroic values and virtues
(usually it refers to the Homeric age and the
heroic characters of the *Iliad* and the *Odyssey*)

Hestia   central cosmic fire, the hearth of the world

homogeneity   property of having parts or qualities of the same
kind and/or equally distributed

hylozoism   the theory that matter includes a self-developing
living force that can produce and reproduce the
living organism, usually without external
intervention

hypostasis   the self-subsistent reality of being
(Plotinus)

hypothetical   a rule of inference based on conditional
syllogism   assumptions

law and nature   the theoretical distinction between human crea-
(sophists)   tions (*nomos*) and natural productions (*phusis*).

like-to-like   the notion that like is perceived by like and that
(principle)   the qualities of the cause are also qualities of the
effect

logic (formal)   discipline that constructs valid forms of
inference

love (Empedocles)   the force that unities things; the creative force in
the universe

material monism   the theory that everything originates from a
single basic material stuff; *see* monism

microdot (material)	matter reduced in the size of a dot
minimalism	reduction to simple and fundamental features
moderation (Aristotle)	a mean between the two extremes of deficiency and excess
monad (Pythagoras)	the divine One, the single formal divine principle of all things
monadology (Leibniz)	theory that the Monads are substantial forms of being and ultimate constructive elements of the universe
monism	the theory that everything originates from a single principle, power or substance
monotheism	the belief in one god
***musica universalis* (Kepler)**	'music of the universe,' the music of the spheres in the Pythagorean tradition
necessity	a reference to 'necessity' can encapsulate the view that all the events are determined by causes whose occurrence is necessitated and hence predetermined
nihilism of modernity (Heidegger)	the forgetfulness of being
not-being	what is not
non-contradiction, law of	the principle that nothing can be both A and not-A at the same time
objectivism (knowledge)	the view that the world exists independently of our comprehension of it
occult science	the systematic research of occult phenomena
omnia in omnibus	everything is in everything
omnipotence	all/infinite/absolute power; usually related to god.
omnipresence	presence in all things; usually related to god.
omniscient	all knowing, having infinite knowledge; usually related to god.
ontology	the study of being or of what is
pantheism	the belief in infinite gods
paradox	a situation that leads to contradictory conclusions, contrary to common-sense or accepted opinion; e.g. the problem of explaining physical motion in Zeno

phenomenology (Husserl)	a school of thought that focuses on the descriptive and introspective analysis of all forms of consciousness and immediate experience
plenum	what is full, the occupied space; all space; opposed to void in early atomic theory
pluralism	the idea that everything originates in a number of basic principles, elements or forces
polymath	person with astounding knowledge in many domains
polytheism	the belief in many gods
potency	the quality of possessing power
potentiality and actuality (Aristotle)	potentiality (or *dunamis*) refers to the capability or possibility of being; actuality (or *energeia*) refers to the actuality of being or the realization of the potentiality of being
predicate (being)	to affirm something about the nature of being
premise	starting point in an argument or inference
presencing **(Heidegger)**	*being present as a being-within-the-world*
primary qualities (Democritus)	qualities that exist in reality, independently of the observer (i.e. the size, shape, order and position of atoms)
principle	source of something; ultimate cause
principle, formal	formative principle, usually immaterial
rationalism	the view that reason is the main source of knowledge
reductio ad absurdum	reduction to the absurd, a method of disproving a proposition by showing that it leads to absurd or untenable conclusions
reincarnation	*metempsychosis*: transmigration, the doctrine that asserts the passage of the soul or spirit into another body after death
relativism (knowledge)	the view that what is known is true only for the knower
rhetoric	the art of persuasive speech and argumentation
secondary qualities (Democritus)	qualities that exist as contents of consciousness (e.g. the color, taste and other apparent qualities of atoms)
self-determination	the idea that human beings are autonomous and able to choose and control their actions

skepticism	state of doubting; a school of thought that promotes suspension of judgement
stimuli (epistemology)	sense data that trigger perception
strife (Empedocles)	the natural force that separates things; the destructive force
subjectivism (epistemology)	the view that all knowledge depends on the knower's subjective mental states
sublime	a feeling or experience of grandeur, nobility and psychic elevation
substance	the real thing that underlies perceptible phenomena
timeless	outside time or temporal duration
uncertainty principle (Heisenberg)	principle that states that the exact position and the exact momentum of subatomic particles cannot be known simultaneously
unlike-to-unlike (principle)	the idea that unlike is perceived by unlike; sense perception occurs through opposite perceptible impressions
vacuum	void, empty space; it was opposed to the plenum of atoms in early atomic theory
virtue ethics	a character-based ethical approach, which focuses on the quality or virtue of the moral agent rather than on duties or on the consequences of the moral action
wisdom	true knowledge; epistemic and psychic cognition of reality

Bibliography

General

Allen, R. E., and Furley, D. (eds.) (1975) *Studies in Presocratic Philosophy*. Routledge: London.

Bailey, C. (1928) *The Greek Atomists and Epicurus*. Clarendon Press: Oxford.

Barnes, J. (1983) *The Presocratic Philosophers*, rev. edn. Routledge: London.

Barnes, J. (1987) *Early Greek Philosophy*. Penguin: London.

Burnet, J. (1930) *Early Greek Philosophy*. Adam & Charles Black: London.

Cherniss, H. F. (1935) *Aristotle's Criticism of Presocratic Philosophy*. Johns Hopkins University Press: Baltimore.

Cleve, F. (1965) *The Giants of Pre-Sophistic Greek Philosophy*, vol. 1. Nijhoff: The Hague.

Curd, P. K., and Graham, D. D. (eds.) (2008) *The Oxford Handbook of Presocratic Philosophy*. Oxford University Press: Oxford.

Curd, P. K., and McKirahan, R. D. (1996) *A Presocratics Reader*. Hackett: Indianapolis.

Diels, H. (1951–2) *Die Fragmente der Vorsokratiker*, 6th edn., revised with additions and index by W. Kranz. Weidmann: Berlin (= DK).

Furley, D. J. (1987) *The Greek Cosmologists*, vol. 1: *The Formation of the Atomic Theory and its Earliest Critics*. Cambridge University Press: Cambridge.

Furley, D. J. (1989) *Cosmic Problems*. Cambridge University Press: Cambridge.

Graham, D. (2010) *The Texts of Early Greek Philosophy: The Complete Fragments and Selected Testimonies of the Major Presocratics*. Cambridge: Cambridge University Press.

Guthrie, W. K. C. (1975) *The Greek Philosophers: From Thales to Aristotle*. Harper & Row: New York.

Introduction to Presocratics: A Thematic Approach to Early Greek Philosophy with Key Readings, First Edition. Giannis Stamatellos.
© 2012 John Wiley & Sons, Inc. Published 2012 by John Wiley & Sons, Inc.

Guthrie, W. K. C. (1962–1965) *A History of Greek Philosophy*, vols. 1–2. Cambridge University Press: Cambridge.

Hussey, E. (1972) *The Presocratics*. Duckworth: London.

Kirk, G. S., Raven, J. E., and Schofield, M. (1983) *The Presocratic Philosophers*, 2nd edn. Cambridge University Press: Cambridge.

Laks, A., and Most, G. (eds.) (1997) *Studies on the Derveni Papyrus*. Clarendon Press: Oxford.

Long, A. A. (ed.) (1999) *The Cambridge Companion to Early Greek Philosophy*. Cambridge University Press: Cambridge.

Mansfeld, J. (1983) *Die Vorsokratiker I*. Reclam: Stuttgart.

Mansfeld, J. (1999) "Sources," in Long (ed.), 22–44.

McKirahan, R. D. (2011) *Philosophy before Socrates: An Introduction with Texts and Commentary*, 2nd edn. Hackett: Indianapolis.

Mourelatos, A. P. D. (ed.) (1974) *The Pre-Socratics: A Collection of Critical Essays*. Anchor Doubleday: New York.

Osborne, C. (2004) *Presocratic Philosophy: A Very Short Introduction*. Oxford University Press: Oxford.

Ring, M. (1987) *Beginning with the Presocratics*. Mayfield: Palo Alto, CA.

Robinson, J. M. (1968) *An Introduction to Early Greek Philosophy*. Cambridge University Press: Cambridge.

Runia, T. D. (2008) "The Sources for Presocratic Philosophy," in Curd and Graham (eds.), 27–54.

Taylor, C. C. W. (ed.) (1997) *Routledge History of Philosophy*, vol. 1: *From the Beginning to Plato*. Routledge: London and New York.

Vamvacas, C. (2009) *The Founders of Western Thought: The Presocratics*. Springer: n.p.

Warburton, N. (2004) *Philosophy: The Basics*, 4th edn. Routledge: London.

Warren, J. (2007) *Presocratics*. Acumen: Stockfield.

Waterfield, R. (2000) *The First Philosophers: The Presocratics and Sophists*. Oxford University Press: Oxford.

West, M. L. (1971) *Early Greek Philosophy and the Orient*. Clarendon Press: Oxford.

Wright, M. R. (1985) *The Presocratics*. Bristol Classical Press: Bristol.

Zeller, E. (1882) *A History of Greek Philosophy from the Earliest Period to the Time of Socrates*, vols. 1–2, trans. S. F. Alleyne. Longmans: London.

Individual Thinkers

Austin, S. (1986) *Parmenides: Being, Bounds and Logic*. Yale University Press: New Haven.

Beaufret, J. (1984) *Parménide: Le Poème*. Michel Chandeigne: La Clayette.

Bollack, J. (1969) *Empédocle*. Les éditions de minuit: Paris.

Conche, M. (1996) *Parménide: Le poème. Fragments*. Presses Universitaires de France: Paris.

Coxon, A. H., and McKirahan, R. D. (ed.) (2009) *The Fragments of Parmenides: A Critical Text with Introduction and Translation*. Parmenides Publishing: Las Vegas, Zurich and Athens.

Curd, P. K. (2004) *The Legacy of Parmenides: Eleatic Monism and Later Presocratic Thought*. Parmenides Publishing: Las Vegas.

Curd, P. K. (2007) *Anaxagoras of Clazomenae*. University of Toronto Press: Toronto.

Gallop, D. (1984) *Parmenides of Elea: Text and Translation with Introduction*. University of Toronto Press: Toronto.

Heitsch, E. (1991) *Parmenides: Die Fragmente*. Artemis Verlag: Munich and Zürich.

Huffman, C. A. (1993) *Philolaus of Croton: Pythagorean and Presocratic*. Cambridge University Press: Cambridge.

Inwood, B. (1992) *The Poem of Empedocles: A Text with an Introduction*. University of Toronto Press: Toronto.

Kahn, C. H. (1960) *Anaximander and the Origins of Greek Cosmology*. Columbia University Press: New York.

Kahn, C. H. (1979) *The Art and Thought of Heraclitus*. Cambridge University Press: Cambridge.

Kahn, C. (2001) *Pythagoras and the Pythagoreans*. Hackett.

Kirk, G. S. (1954) *Heraclitus: The Cosmic Fragments*. Cambridge University Press: Cambridge.

Lesher, J. (1992) *Xenophanes of Colophon, Fragments: A Text and Translation with a Commentary*. University of Toronto Press: Toronto.

Marcovich, M. (1967) *Heraclitus: Greek Text with a Short Commentary*. The Los Andes University Press: Merida, Venezuela.

Martin, A., and Primavesi, O. (1998), *L'Empédocle de Strasbourg*. Walter de Gruyter: Berlin and New York.

Mourelatos, A. P. D. (2008) *The Route of Parmenides: Revised and Expanded Edition*. Parmenides Publishing: Las Vegas.

O'Brien D., and Frère, J. (1987) *Le Poème de Parménide*. J. Vrin: Paris.

Philip, J. A. (1966) *Pythagoras and Early Pythagorianism*. University of Toronto Press: Toronto.

Robinson, T. M. (1987) *Heraclitus, Fragments: A Text and Translation with a Commentary*. University of Toronto Press: Toronto.

Roussos, E. N. (2000) *ΗΡΑΚΛΕΙΤΟΣ*, vol. 2. Stigmi: Athens.

Roussos, E. N. (2002) *ΠΑΡΜΕΝΙΔΗΣ*, vol. 3. Stigmi: Athens.

Roussos, E. N. (2007) *ΕΜΠΕΔΟΚΛΗΣ*, vol. 4. Stigmi: Athens.

Roussos, E. N. (2010), *ΦΕΡΕΚΥΔΗΣ Ο ΣΥΡΙΟΣ*. Centre International de Recherche Ésope – La Fontaine: Athens.

Schofield, M. (1980) *An Essay of Anaxagoras*. Cambridge University Press: Cambridge.

Schibli, H. S. (1990) *Pherecydes of Syros*. Clarendon Press: Oxford.

Sider, D. (2005) *The Fragments of Anaxagoras. Introduction, Text, and Commentary.* 2nd edn. Academia Verlag: Sankt Augustin.

Tarán, L. (1965) *Parmenides: A Text with Translation, Commentary and Critical Essays.* Princeton University Press: Princeton.

Taylor, C. C. W. (1999) *The Atomists: Leucippus and Democritus. A Text and Translation with a Commentary.* University of Toronto Press: Toronto.

Wright, M. R. (1981) *Empedocles: The Extant Fragments.* Yale University Press: New Haven.

Wright, M. R. (1997) "Empedocles," in Taylor (ed.), 75–207.

Studies and Themes

Adkins, A. H. A. (1980) "The Greek Concept of Justice from Homer to Plato," *Classical Philology* 75: 256–268.

Algra, K. (1999) "The Beginnings of Cosmology," in Long (ed.), 45–65.

Baltussen, H. (2000) *Theophrastus against the Presocratics and Plato: Peripatetic Dialectic in the De Sensibus.* Brill: Leiden.

Barnes, J. (1979) "Parmenides and the Eleatic One," *Archiv für Geschichte der Philosophie* 61: 1–21.

Benveniste, E. (1932) "Grec ψυχή," *Bulletin de la Société de Linguistique de Paris* 33: 165–8.

Bremmer, J. (1983) *The Early Greek Concept of Soul.* Princeton University Press: Princeton.

Broadie, S. (1999) "Rational Theology," in Long (ed.), 205–224.

Burkert, W. (1972) *Lore and Science in Ancient Pythagorianism.* Cambridge University Press: Cambridge.

Chalmers, W. R. (1960) "Parmenides and the Beliefs of Mortals," *Phronesis* 5: 5–22.

Clark, R. J. (1969) "Parmenides and Sense-Perception," *Revue des Études Grecques* 82: 14–32.

Cornford, F. M. (1974) "Mysticism and Science in the Pythagorean Tradition," in Mourelatos (ed.), 35–160.

Cornford, F. M. (1975) "Anaxagoras' Theory of Matter," in Allen and Furley (eds.), 275–322.

Curd, P. K. (1991) "Knowledge and Unity in Heraclitus," *The Monist* 74: 531–49.

Curd, P. K. (2002) "The Metaphysics of Physics: Mixture and Separation in Empedocles and Anaxagoras," in V. Caston and D. Graham (eds.) *Presocratic Philosophy: Essays in Honour of Alexander Mourelatos.* Ashgate: London, 139–158.

Curd, P. K. (2008) "Anaxagoras and the Theory of Everything," in Curd and Graham (eds.), 230–249.

Dancy, R. M. (1989) "Thales, Anaximander, and Infinity," *Apeiron* 22: 149–190.

Darcus, S. (1974) "Daimon as a Force Shaping Ethos in Heraclitus," *Phoenix* 28: 390–407.

Darcus, S. (1979) "A Person's Relation to ψυχή in Homer, Hesiod and the Greek Lyric Poets," *Glotta* 57: 30–39.

Engman, J. (1991) "Cosmic Justice in Anaximander," *Phronesis* 36: 1–25.

Fränkel, H. (1942) "Zeno of Elea's Attacks on Plurality," *The American Journal of Philology* 63.1: 1–25 (Part 1); 63.2: 193–206 (Part 2).

Fränkel, H. (1974a) "A Thought Pattern in Heraclitus," in Mourelatos (ed.), 214–228.

Fränkel, H. (1974b) "Xenophanes' Empiricism and His Critique of Knowledge (B34)," in Mourelatos (ed.), 118–131.

Frede, M. (2008) "Aristotle's Account of the Origins of Philosophy," in Curd and Graham (eds.), 501–529.

Frinkelberg, A. (1993) "Anaximander's Conception of the Apeiron," *Phronesis* 28: 229–256.

Furley, D. J. (1957) "Empedocles and the Clepsydra," *Journal of Hellenic Studies* 77: 31–34.

Furley, D. J. (1974a) "Zeno and Invisible Magnitudes," in Mourelatos (ed.), 353–367.

Furley, D. J. (1974b) "The Atomists' Reply to the Eleatics," in Mourelatos (ed.), 504–526.

Furth, M. (1974) "Elements of Eleatic Ontology," in Mourelatos (ed.), 241–270.

Glazebrook, T. (2001) "Zeno against Mathematical Physics," *Journal of the History of Ideas* 62: 193–210.

Gottschalk, H. P. (1971) "Soul as *harmonia*," *Phronesis* 16: 179–198.

Graham, D. W. (1999) "Empedocles and Anaxagoras: Responses to Parmenides," in Long (ed.), 159–180.

Graham, D. W. (2006) *Exploring the Cosmos: The Ionian Tradition of Scientific Philosophy*. Princeton University Press: Princeton.

Greene, W. C. (1936) "Fate, Good and Evil in Pre-Socratic Philosophy," *Harvard Studies in Classical Philology* 47: 85–129.

Guthrie, W. K. C. (1974) "Flux and *Logos* in Heraclitus," in Mourelatos (ed.), 197–213.

Hankinson, R. J. (2008) "Reason, Cause, and Explanation in Presocratic Philosophy," in Curd and Graham (eds.), 434–457.

Heidel, W. A. (1974) "Qualitive Change in Pre-Socratic Philosophy," in Mourelatos (ed.), 86–95.

Herman, A. (2004) *To Think Like God: Pythagoras, Parmenides and the Origins of Philosophy*. Parmenides: Chicago, IL.

Huffman, C. (1988) "The Role of Number in Philolaus' Philosophy," *Phronesis* 33: 1–30.

Huffman, C. A. (1999) "The Pythagorean Tradition," in Long (ed.), 46–87.

Hussey, E. (1982) "Epistemology and Meaning in Heraclitus," in Schofield and Nussbaum (eds.), 1–32.

Hussey, E. (1990) "The Beginnings of Epistemology: From Homer to Philolaos," in Everson, S. (ed.), *Epistemology*. Cambridge: Cambridge University Press, 11–38.

Hussey, E. (1991) "Heraclitus on Living and Dying," *The Monist* 74: 517–530.

Jameson, G. (1958) "Well-Rounded Truth and Circular Thought in Parmenides," *Phronesis* 3: 15–30.

Kahn, Ch. H. (2003) "Presocratic Greek Ethics," in L. C. Becker and C. B. Becker (eds.) *A History of Western Ethics*. Routledge: London, 1–8.

Kingsley, P. (1995) *Ancient Philosophy, Mystery, and Magic: Empedocles and the Pythagorean Tradition*. Oxford University Press: Oxford.

Kirk, G. S. (1949) "Heraclitus and Death in Battle," *American Journal of Philology* 70: 384–393.

Kirk, G. S. (1951) "Natural Change in Heraclitus," *Mind* 60: 384–393.

Laks, A. (1993) "Mind's Crisis: On Anaxagoras' *nous*," *Southern Journal of Philosophy* 31: 19–38.

Laks, A. (1999) "Soul, Sensation and Thought," in Long (ed.), 250–270.

Lear, J. (1981) "A Note on Zeno's Arrow," *Phronesis* 26: 91–104.

Lesher, J. H. (1981) "Perceiving and Knowing in the Iliad and Odyssey," *Phronesis* 26: 2–24.

Lesher, J. H. (1999) "Early Interest in Knowledge," in Long (ed.), 225–249.

Lesher, J. H. (2008) "The Humanizing Knowledge in Presocratic Thought," in Curd and Graham (eds.), 458–484.

Lloyd, G. E. R. (1964) "Hot and Cold, Dry and Wet in Early Greek Thought," *Journal of Hellenic Studies* 84: 92–106.

Lloyd, G. E. R. (1992) *Polarity and Analogy: Two Types of Argumentation in Early Greek Thought*. Bristol Classical Press: Bristol.

Long, A. A. (1974) "Empedocles' Cosmic Cycle in the Sixties," in Mourelatos (ed.), 397–425.

Longrigg, J. (1985) "Elements and after: A Study in Pre-Socratic Physics of the Second Half of the Fifth Century," *Apeiron* 19: 93–115.

McDiarmid, J. B. (1953) "Theophrastus on the Presocratic Causes," *Harvard Studies in Classical Philology* 61: 85–156.

McKirahan, R. D. (1999) "Zeno," in Long (ed.), 134–158.

McKirahan, R. D. (2008) "Signs and Arguments in Parmenides B8," in Curd and Graham (eds.), 189–229.

Miller, F. D., Jr. (1977) "Parmenides on Mortal Belief," *Journal of the History of Philosophy* 15: 253–265.

Minar, L. (1963) "Cosmic Periods in the Philosophy of Empedocles," *Phronesis* 8: 127–145.

Mourelatos, A. P. D. (1974) "The Deceptive Words of Parmenides' 'Doxa,'" in Mourelatos (ed.), 293–311.

Mourelatos, A. P. D. (2008) "The Cloud-Astrophysics of Xenophanes and Ionian Material Monism," in Curd and Graham (eds.), 134–168.

Nussbaum, M. C. (1972) "ψυχή in Heraclitus," *Phronesis* 17: 1–16, 153–170.

O'Brien, D. (1969) *Empedocles' Cosmic Cycle.* Cambridge University Press: Cambridge.

Owen, G. E. L. (1960) "Eleatic Questions," *Classical Quarterly* 10: 84–102.

Owen, G. E. L. (1966) "Plato and Parmenides on the Timeless Present," *The Monist* 50: 317–340.

Pachenko, D. (1993) "Thales and the Origin of Theoretical Reasoning," *Configurations* 3: 387–484.

Palmer, J. (1999) *Plato's Reception of Parmenides.* Oxford University Press: Oxford.

Palmer, J. (2008) "Classical Representations and the Use of Presocratics," in Curd and Graham (eds.), 530–554.

Peck, A. L. (1926) "Anaxagoras and the Parts," *Classical Quarterly* 20: 57–71.

Phillips, E. D. (1955) "Parmenides on Thought and Being," *Philosophical Review* 64: 15–29.

Primavesi, O. (2008) "Empedocles: Physical and Mythical Divinity," in Curd and Graham (eds.), 250–283.

Puhvel, J. (1976) "The Origins of Greek Kosmos and Latin Mundus," *American Journal of Philology* 97: 154–167.

Raven, J. E. (1954) "The Basis of Anaxagoras' Cosmology," *Classical Quarterly* 4: 123–137.

Robb, K. (1968) "Psyche and Logos in the Fragments of Heraclitus: The Origins of the Concept of the Soul," *The Monist* 69: 315–351.

Robinson, T. M. (1968) "Heraclitus on Soul," *The Monist* 69: 305–313.

Robinson, T. M. (2008) "Presocratic Theology," in Curd and Graham (eds.), 485–498.

Sandywell, B. (1996) *Presocratic Reflexivity: The Construction of Philosophical Discourse.* London and New York: Routledge.

Sedley, D. (1999) "Parmenides and Melissus," in Long (ed.), 113–133.

Seligman, P. (1978) "Soul and Cosmos in Presocratic Philosophy," *Dionysius* 2: 5–17.

Smith, C. I. (1966) "Heraclitus and Fire," *Journal of the History of Ideas* 27: 125–127.

Solmsen, Fr. (1950) "Chaos and Apeiron," *Studi Italiani de Filologia Classica* 24: 235–248.

Stokes, M. C. (1971) *One and Many in Presocratic Philosophy.* Harvard University Press – Center for Hellenic Studies: Cambridge, MA.

Strang, C. (1975) "The Physical Theory of Anaxagoras," *Archiv für Gesschichte der Philosophie* 45: 101–118.

Teodorsson, S. (1982) *Anaxagoras'Theory of Matter.* Acta Universitatis: Göteborg.

Trépanier, S. (2003) "Empedocles on the Ultimate Symmetry of the World," *Oxford Studies in Ancient Philosophy* 24: 1–58.

Tugwell, S. (1964) "The Way of Truth," *Classical Quarterly* 14: 36–41.

Vlastos, G. (1953) "Isonomia," *American Journal of Philology* 74: 337–366.

Vlastos, G. (1974a) "The Physical Theory of Anaxagoras," in Mourelatos (ed.), 459–488.

Vlastos, G. (1974b) "Equality and Justice in the Early Greek Cosmologies," *Classical Philology* 42: 156–178.

Vlastos, G. (1975) "Ethics and Physics in Democritus," in Allen and Furley (eds.), 381–408.

Wright, M. R. (2008) "Presocratic Cosmologies," in Curd and Graham (eds.), 413–433.

Other Sources

Adamson, P. (2002) *The Arabic Plotinus: A Philosophical Study of the "Theology of Aristotle."* Duckworth: London.

Adkins, A. H. A. (1972) *Moral Values and Political Behaviour in Ancient Greece.* Chatto and Windus: London.

Adorno, T., and Tiedemann, R. (2002) *Metaphysics: Concept and Problems.* Stanford University Press: Stanford.

Badiou, A. (2006) "Lacan and the Pre-Socratics," in *lacan.com* at: http://www.lacan.com/badpre.htm <last access: 10/12/2010>

Bishop, P. (2004) *Nietzsche and Antiquity.* Camden House: Rochester, NY.

Cairns, D. L. (1993) *Aidos: The Psychology and Ethics of Honour and Shame in Ancient Greek Literature.* Oxford: Clarendon.

Catana, L. (2005) *The Concept of Contraction in Giordano Bruno's Philosophy.* Ashgate: Aldershot.

Charles, S., and Skinner, Q. (eds.) (1988) *The Cambridge History of Renaissance Philosophy.* Cambridge University Press: Cambridge and New York.

Claus, D. (1981) *Towards the Soul.* Yale University Press: New Haven and London.

Cohen, I. B. (1983) *The Newtonian Revolution.* Cambridge University Press: Cambridge.

Cooper, J. M. (1999) *Reason and Emotion: Essays in Ancient Moral Psychology and Ethical Theory.* Princeton University Press: Princeton.

Cox, C. (1999) *Nietzsche: Naturalism and Interpretation.* University of California Press: Berkley.

Deleuze, G. (2006) *Nietzsche and Philosophy.* Continuum: London & New York.

Dillon, J. (1977) *The Middle Platonists.* Duckworth: London.

Dodds, E. R. (1951) *The Greeks and the Irrational.* University of California Press: Berkley and Los Angeles.

Eliade, M. (1949) *Le Mythe de l'éternel retour*. Gallimard: Paris.

Everson, S. (ed.) *Companions to Ancient Thought I: Epistemology*. Cambridge University Press: Cambridge.

Ferguson, J. (1958) *Moral Values in the Ancient World*. Methuen: London.

Feyerabend, P., and Terpstra, B. (1999) *Conquest of Abundance*. University of Chicago Press: Chicago.

Fischer, N. (1992) *Hybris: A Study in the Values of Honour and Shame in Ancient Greece*. Aris & Philips: Warminster.

Freeman, K. (1952) *God, Man and State: Greek Concepts*. Macdonald: London.

Freud, S. (1961) "Analysis Terminable and Interminable" [1937], in Strachey, J. (ed.) *The Standard Edition of the Complete Psychological Works of Sigmund Freud*, vol. 23. Hogarth Press: London, 209–254.

Furley, D. J. (1956) "The Early History of the Concept of Soul," *Bulletin of the Institute of Classical Studies* 3: 1–18.

Gerson, L. P. (1990) *God and Greek Philosophy*. Routledge: London.

Gregory, J. (2005) *A Companion to Greek Tragedy*. Wiley-Blackwell: Oxford.

Hallward, P. (2003) *Badiou: A Subject to Truth*. University of Minnesota Press: Minneapolis.

Hankins, J. (2007) *The Cambridge Companion to Renaissance Philosophy*. Cambridge University Press: Cambridge.

Hankinson, R. J. (1999) *Cause and Explanation in Ancient Greek Thought*. Clarendon Press: Oxford.

Hartnack, J. (1998) *An Introduction to Hegel's Logic*. Hackett: Cambridge, MA.

Havelock, E. A. (1978) *The Greek Concept of Justice: From Its Shadow in Homer to Its Substance in Plato*. Harvard University Press: Cambridge.

Heidegger, M., and Fink, E. (1970) *Heraclitus Seminar*, trans. H. Seibert. The University of Alabama Press: Alabama.

Heisenberg, W. (1989) *Physics and Philosophy*. Penguin: New York.

Huby, P. (1967) *Greek Ethics*. Macmillan: London.

Hyland, D. A., and Manoussakis, J. P. (2006) *Heidegger and the Greeks: Interpretive Essays*. Indiana University Press: Bloomington, IN.

Jacobs, D. C. (1999) *The Presocratics After Heidegger*. State University of New York Press: Albany.

Jung, C. G. (1973) *Memories, Dreams and Reflections*. Pantheon Books: New York.

Kahn, Ch. H. (1973) *The Verb "Be" in Ancient Greek*. Reidel: Dordrecht.

Lassale, F. (1858) *Die Philosophie Herakleitos' des Dunklen von Ephesos*. Duncker: Berlin.

MacIntyre, A. (1985) *After Virtue*, 2nd edn. Notre Dame: University of Notre Dame Press.

Mansfeld, J., and De Rijk, L. M. (1975) *Kephalion: Studies in Greek Philosophy and its Continuation Offered to Professor C. J. de Vogel*. Van Gorcum: Assen.

Melchert, N. (2010) *The Great Conversation: A Historical Introduction to Philosophy*. Oxford University Press: Oxford.

Merleau-Ponty, M., Johnson, G. A., and Smith, M. B. (1993) *The Merleau-Ponty Aesthetics Reader: Philosophy and Painting.* Northwestern University Press: Evanston, IL.

Morgan, M. L. (2002) *Spinoza: Complete Works,* trans. S. Shirley. Hackett: Indianapolis and Cambridge.

Naddaf, G. (2005) *The Greek Concept of Nature.* State University of New York Press: Albany.

O'Connell, E. (2006) *Heraclitus and Derrida: Presocratic Deconstruction.* Peter Lang: New York.

Onians, R. B. (1954) *The Origins of European Thought.* Cambridge: Cambridge University Press.

Onley, J. (1980) *The Rhizome and the Flower: The Perennial Philosophy, Yeats and Jung.* University of California Press: Berkeley.

Popper, Karl R. (1998) *The World of Parmenides.* Routledge: London and New York.

Roussos, E. N. (2010) *ΣΥΜΒΟΛΗ ΣΤΗΝ ΒΙΒΛΙΟΓΡΑΦΙΑ ΤΗΣ ΠΡΟΣΩΚΡΑΤΙΚΗΣ ΕΝΝΟΙΟΛΟΓΙΑΣ.* Academy of Athens: Athens.

Sambursky, S. (1956) *The Physical World of the Greeks,* trans. Merton Dagut. Macmillan: New York.

Schofield, M., and Nussbaum, M. C. (eds.) (1982) *Language and Logos: Studies in Ancient Greek Philosophy.* Cambridge University Press: Cambridge.

Smith, A. (2004) *Philosophy in Late Antiquity.* Routledge: London and New York.

Sorabji, R. (1980) *Necessity, Cause and Blame.* London: Duckworth.

Sorabji, R. (1983) *Time, Creation and the Continuum: Theories in Antiquity and the Early Middle Ages.* Duckworth: London.

Stamatellos, G. (2007) *Plotinus and the Presocratics.* State University of New York Press: Albany.

Weinberger, E. (ed.) (1999) *Jorge Luis Borges: Selected Non-Fiction.* Penguin: New York.

Wilkerson, D. (2006) *Nietzsche and the Greeks.* Continuum: London.

Williams, H. L. (1989) *Hegel, Heraclitus and Marx's Dialectic.* Harvester Wheatsheaf: Hemel Hempstead.

Wright, M. R. (1995) *Cosmology in Antiquity.* Routledge: London and New York.

Wright, M. R. (ed.) (2000) *Reason and Necessity: Essays on Plato's Timaeus.* London: Duckworth.

Wright, M. R. (2009) *Introducing Greek Philosophy.* Acumen: Durham.

Zuntz, G. (1971) *Persephone: Three Essays on Religion and Thought in Magna Graecia.* Oxford University Press: Oxford.

Index

Introduction to Presocratics: A Thematic Approach to Early Greek Philosophy
with Key Readings, First Edition. Giannis Stamatellos.
© 2012 John Wiley & Sons, Inc. Published 2012 by John Wiley & Sons, Inc.

Index compiled by Frank Pert